Dedication

To my husband Ed, with love. Thanks for hiking with me, giving me shuttle rides, reading my manuscripts, and providing honest criticism.

MAUI
TRAILS

*Walks, Strolls and Treks
on the Valley Isle*

Kathy Morey

WILDERNESS PRESS
BERKELEY

Library of Congress Card Number 91-22224
ISBN 0-89997-125-3

Manufactured in the United States of America
Published by Wilderness Press
    2440 Bancroft Way
    Berkeley, CA 94704
    (415) 843-8080
    Write or call for free catalog

♻ Printed on recycled paper with soybean ink

Library of Congress Cataloging-in-Publication Data

Morey, Kathy.
    Maui trails : walks, strolls, and treks on the valley isle / by
Kathy Morey.
       p.   cm.
    Includes bibliographical references and index.
    ISBN 0-89997-125-3
    1. Maui (Hawaii)--Description and travel--Guide-books. 2. Hiking-
-Hawaii--Maui. I. Title.
DU628.M3M67 1991
919.69'21--dc20   91-22224
                                                      CIP

Table of Contents

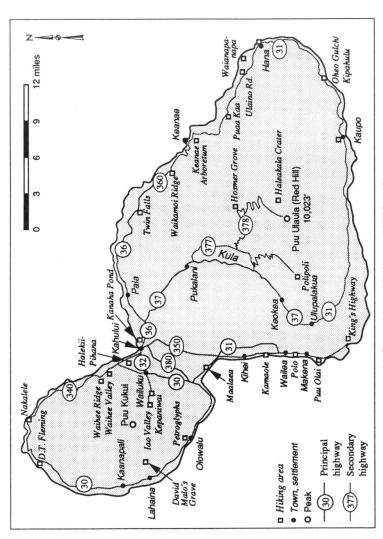

Maui: Overview of Principal Hiking Areas

N

0   3   6   9   12 miles

Nakalele

D.T. Fleming

340

Waihee Ridge
Waihee Valley
Puu Kukui
Iao Valley
Kepaniwai
Petroglyphs

Kaanapali

Lahaina

David
Malo's
Grave

Olowalu

30

Halekii-
Pihana

Wailuku

32

380

30

350

31

Maalaea

Kahului
Kanaha Pond

36

Paia

37

36

360

Twin Falls

Waikamoi Ridge

Keanae

Keanae
Arboretum

377

Kula

378

Hosmer Grove

Puaa Kaa

Ulaino Rd.

Waianapa-
napa

Hana

31

Pukalani

Haleakala Crater

Puu Ulaula (Red Hill)
10,023'

Polipoli

Ulupalakua

Keokea

37

31

King's Highway

Kaupo

Oheo Gulch/
Kipahulu

Kihei

Kamaole
Wailea
Polo
Makena
Puu Olai

□ *Hiking area*

● *Town, settlement*

○ *Peak*

30 —— Principal
highway

377 —— Secondary
highway

Introduction

"Maui? What do I know about Maui? Nothing! I just own a condo there."

What a shame! Maui is an island of overwhelming beauty and of great contrasts; it defies the mind's attempts to take it all in. It's a large island whose shape, rugged terrain, and road conditions defy the driver's attempts to see it by car. A drive around it or a flight over it may satisfy the eyes, but it denies the other senses their experiences: the fragrance of yellow ginger, the sound of rainforest bamboo rattling in the breeze, the feeling of warm sand underfoot, the sharp taste of wild guavas.

You can't experience Maui fully from a condo or even from a vehicle. The best of the island is outside, along the trails, where there's nothing to separate you from the immediate sensory experience, even sensory overload, of Maui. You don't have to walk far: a worthwhile hike on Maui can be as short as a quarter-mile stroll suitable for anyone who's ambulatory, or it can be as long as a three-day backpack in Haleakala's crater. How do I know? I walked every trail that's used as a trip in this book at least once in the summer and fall of 1990.

The shape of things. Maui consists of a west lobe and an east lobe connected by an isthmus. Maui's older, smaller, west lobe, West Maui, is a single volcano whose flanks have eroded into deep valleys and knife-thin ridges. Its upper slopes and cloud-covered peak harbor a nearly impenetrable swamp. Maui's younger, much larger east lobe, East Maui, is also a single volcano, Haleakala. On Haleakala's vast flanks are rainforests, huge cattle ranches, parched deserts of jagged lava, and native dryland forests. Erosion has carved immense stream valleys into Haleakala. Two of the largest of those valleys meet atop Haleakala to form what's commonly referred to as Haleakala's "crater." Long white beaches backed by thorny *kiawe* trees face bays of turquoise water on the drier west and south shores of West and East Maui. The north and east slopes are covered by rainforests and corrugated by steep cliffs and deep gullies. Between West and East Maui lies a low, sandy isthmus where business and industry are concentrated. Broad fields of pineapple and sugarcane carpet the isthmus and the drier slopes of both volcanoes.

1

Take time for Maui. It takes time to see Maui, partly because there's so much to see and partly because most of the tourist accommodations are far from the major scenic areas (including the best hiking areas). The resorts are concentrated almost exclusively on the west shore of West Maui (Lahaina, Kaanapali, and Kapalua) and on the southwest shore of East Maui (Kihei, Wailea, and Makena). There are some very good hikes scattered near the resorts. However, the only major scenic and hiking area that's "convenient" to the resorts is Iao Valley State Park. The resorts are a long way from scenic areas like Haleakala National Park, Hana town and the road to it, and the Oheo Gulch/Kipahulu District of Haleakala National Park.[1]

If you have only a day or two on Maui, stay put and enjoy what's nearby. There's probably a short hike or two in this book that will be very near you. Come back for a longer visit when you can!

If possible, stay a week or two on Maui. Allow at least half a day to visit Iao Valley State Park. Allow a full day to visit Haleakala's summit area; realize that you'll spend about half of it driving. If you want to drive to Hana, plan to stay at least one night in or near Hana, at least two nights if you also wish to visit Kipahulu.[2] Backpackers will probably want to spend three nights—the maximum allowed in any 30-day period—in Haleakala's crater, though three nights (or, rather, the four days around them) are barely enough to see the entire crater.

Be a good visitor. Traffic and crowding near resort and urban areas can be as bad as on the mainland. Developers in resort areas are bulldozing the wild, natural Maui into a tame, plastic Maui almost faster than Maui natives can get out of the way. Local people may (understandably) worry that if they stand still too long, they'll be 'dozed, too. In these areas, even in once-remote Hana, the *aloha*

---

[1] Oheo Gulch/Kipahulu was for a time referred to as "Seven Sacred Pools," a name that seems to have been a travel promoter's thoughtless invention. There are more than seven pools, and none was ever sacred. The Park Service refers to the area as the Kipahulu District; when I say "Kipahulu," I mean the Kipahulu District of Haleakala National Park. (There's also a tiny Kipahulu village beyond the Kipahulu District of Haleakala National Park.)

[2] A few tourist accommodations, including budget accommodations in Hana, exist outside the resort areas. See J. D. Bisignani's *Hawaii Handbook* (in the Bibliography) for more information—though the prices may be out of date. Bed-and-breakfast accommodations exist, too. See also Appendix A, Camping on Maui, in this book.

spirit seems tattered. Hawaii is not Paradise. Paradise is infinite and self-renewing. Hawaii is a real place of finite space and resources, where real people live real lives with jobs, families, budgets, and bills. Hawaii needs loving care from its visitors as well as from its natives. As the number of tourists increases, I think it becomes important that we visitors actively contribute to the *aloha* spirit instead of just passively expecting to receive it. Bring your best manners and your patience with you to Maui. Be the first to smile and wave. Be the first to pull your car over (safely) so that someone else can pass. Be scrupulous in observing the rules of the trail in order to help preserve what's left of Maui's vanishing wild places. NO TRESPASSING, KEEP OUT, or KAPU ("forbidden") signs mean, "You stay out." Please respect those signs.

Pool beside Ulaino Road

Getting Information About Maui

The search for the perfect trail guide. I wish I could be certain this was a flawless book. However, some things limit an author's ability to produce a perfect, error-free, always up-to-date book. Here are some of the factors, and what you can do to help yourself (and me).

Nature makes constant revisions; so do agencies. Nature constantly reshapes the landscape across which we plan to trek. That's usually a gradual process, but once in a while she makes drastic changes overnight. A landslide can erase a trail in seconds. Erosion can undercut a cliff edge and make last year's safe hike an extremely dangerous one, so that the local authorities close a trail you'd hoped to ramble on. And Maui's fragile volcanic terrain erodes quite rapidly.

Agencies in charge of hiking areas may close an area because they've realized it's environmentally too sensitive to withstand more human visits. An area once open to overnight camping may become a day-use-only area. Trails become impassable from lack of maintenance. Happily, agencies may open new areas because they've been able to acquire new acreage or complete a trail-building project.

Change is the only thing that's constant in this world, so that guidebook authors and publishers always play "catch up" with Nature and with agencies. We want to keep guidebooks up to date, but we are always at least one step behind the latest changes. The day when you'll have constantly revised books on-line at your wristwatch/computer terminal isn't here yet. So it's possible that a few trail descriptions are becoming obsolete even as this book goes to press.

Write for the latest information. It's a good idea to use this book in conjunction with the latest information from the agency in charge of the areas you plan to hike in. However, I must regretfully tell you that as of this writing, the recreation map of Maui published by the Maui District of the Divisions of Forestry and Wildlife and State Parks, dated March 1986, is badly out of date and seriously lacking in trail information for hikers. There isn't a better map available from those agencies. I've been told it's being updated; I hope that *you* get the updated version and that it's more helpful. This book gives you a far more complete and detailed picture of Maui's principal hiking and backcountry camping opportunities than the current recreation map does. And it describes those opportunities from a hiker's perspective.

Still, it's a good idea to write to these agencies as soon as you've read this book and decided where you want to hike and camp on Maui. Ask them for their latest trail and camping maps, regulations, and permit-issuing procedures. Except for Haleakala National Park, enclose a stamped, self-addressed envelope for *your* convenience in getting the information you need as soon as possible. (National parks almost always use the franking privilege of Federal agencies, so you'd be wasting a stamp.) Their addresses and telephone numbers are in "Getting Permits or Permission."

Prepare yourself with general information, too. A generous source of a wide variety of useful information about Hawaii is the Hawaii Visitors Bureau. Here are the addresses of their offices on the mainland:

Canada: 4915 Cedar Crescent, Delta, B.C. V4M 1J9, Canada

Chicago: Suite 1031, 180 North Michigan Avenue, Chicago, IL 60601

Los Angeles: Room 502, Central Plaza, 3440 Wilshire Boulevard, Los Angeles, CA 90010

New York: Room 1407, 441 Lexington Avenue, New York, NY 10017

San Francisco: Suite 450, 50 California Street, San Francisco, CA 94111

Washington, D.C.: Suite 519, 1511 K Street N.W., Washington, D.C., 20005

A letter to them will get you a fat packet full of all kinds of handy information.

Let me know what you think and what you find. I hope this book helps make your visit to Maui even more enjoyable than it would have been. I plan to update it regularly, and you can help me. Let me know what you think of it. Did you find it helpful when you visited Maui? Was it accurate and complete enough that you enjoyed the walks and hikes you took based on the book? Did you notice any significant discrepancies between this book and what you found when you visited Maui, discrepancies that you judge are not just the result of two different perceptions of the same thing? What were they? The publisher and I are very concerned about accuracy. We'd appreciate your comments. I'd also like to know about it if you think there are ways in which the book can be improved. Write to me in care of Wilderness Press, 2440 Bancroft Way, Berkeley, CA 94704.

Spoken Hawaiian: An Incomplete and Unauthoritative Guide

What, only 12 letters?! Nineteenth-century American missionaries used only 12 letters to create a written version of the spoken Hawaiian language. Superficially, that might make Hawaiian seem simple. But Hawaiian is a much more complex and subtle language than 12 letters can do justice to. However, we're stuck with those 12 letters—the five English vowels (a, e, i, o, u) and seven of the consonants (h, k, l, m, n, p, w).

Consonants. The consonants have the same sound in Hawaiian as they do in your everyday English except for "w." "W" is sometimes pronounced as "v" when it follows "a," always pronounced as "v" when it follows "e" or "i."

Vowels. The vowels are generally pronounced as they are in Italian, with each vowel sounded separately. Authentic Hawaiian makes further distinctions, but those are of more interest to scholars than to hikers.[1] The following is a simplified system. Vowel sounds in general are:

a	like "ah" in "Ah!"
e	like "ay" in "day."
i	like "ee" as in "whee!"
o	like "o" in "go."
u	like "oo" in "food" (or "u" in "rude").

Notice that that means that when you see two or more of the

---

[1] Remember that Hawaiian evolved as a spoken, not a written, language. Authentic written Hawaiian uses two special marks to indicate other variations on pronouncing vowels in spoken Hawaiian. Those variations change the meaning of a word. One is the glottal stop, indicated by a single quotation mark ('). It indicates that you should make a complete break in your voice before sounding the vowel that follows it. There really isn't an English equivalent, though the break in "uh-oh!" is close. Another is the macron mark, which is a straight line over a vowel. It indicates that you should pronounce a vowel as a long sound instead of a short sound. For example, the Hawaiian long-a sound is "ah," and the Hawaiian short-a sound is "uh." We have the same sounds in English but don't use special marks to distinguish between them except in dictionaries. Road signs, topographic maps, and this book don't use glottal stops or macron marks.

same letter in a row, you pronounce each of them separately:
"Kaanapali" is Ka-a-na-pa-li (but everyone pronounces it "Ka-na-pa-li").
"Waihee" is Wai-he-e.
"Piilani" is Pi-i-la-ni.
"Hookipa" is Ho-o-ki-pa.
"Puu" is Pu-u.

That seems *too* simple, and it is. If you tried to pronounce every vowel, speaking Hawaiian would turn into a nightmare. You wouldn't live long enough to pronounce some words. Fortunately, several pairs of vowels often—but not always—form merged sounds.

Vowel Pairs Whose Sounds Merge. Like every other language, Hawaiian has vowel pairs whose sounds naturally "smooth" into each other. They're similar to Italian or English diphthongs. The degree to which the two sounds are merged in Hawaiian is officially less than occurs in English, but most Hawaiian people I've talked with merge them fully. Vowel-pair pronunciation is approximately:

ae	often smoothed to "eye" as in "*eye*ful" or "i" in "*i*ce." It's the English long-i sound.
ai	often smoothed as for "ae," above.
ao	often smoothed to sound like "ow" in "*cow*."
au	often smoothed to "ow" in "*cow*", too.
ei	sometimes smoothed to "ay" as in "d*ay*." It's the English long-a sound.
eu	smooth the sounds together a little, like "ayoo."
oi	usually like "oi" in "*oi*l"—in other words, just what you're used to.

Syllables. Every Hawaiian syllable ends in a vowel sound. A Hawaiian syllable never contains more than one consonant. That means every consonant goes with the vowel that *follows* it. Every vowel not preceded by a consonant stands alone when you break a *written* word into syllables (you may smooth some of them together when you *speak*). For example:

"Aa" consists of the two syllables a-a (it's a kind of lava flow).
"Kihei" consists of the three syllables Ki-he-i (but everyone pronounces it "KEE-hay").
"Kipahulu" consists of the four syllables Ki-pa-hu-lu (an area famed for its cascades, falls, and natural swimming pools, now part of Haleakala National Park)
"Haleakala" consists of the five syllables Ha-le-a-ka-la (the dormant volcano that makes up East Maui; the national park that encompasses its upper slopes and a strip of its southeast flank).
"Ulupalakua" consists of the six syllables U-lu-pa-la-ku-a (a huge ranch on the southwest slopes of Haleakala; home of Maui's only winery, Tedeschi Winery).

"Liliuokalani" consists of the seven syllables Li-li-u-o-ka-la-ni (Hawaii's last monarch and writer of the beloved song "Aloha Oe").

Accent. In general, the accent falls on the next-to-last syllable for words with three or more syllables and on the first syllable for words of two syllables. For words of more than three syllables, you put a little stress on every other syllable preceding the accented one. Don't worry about this; it seems to come naturally.

There are common-usage exceptions, such as makai (ma-KAI, with the accent on the last syllable). When you see exceptions such as those, chances are that what has happened is that European usage has fully merged two sounds into one. Proper Hawaiian pronunciation of makai would be closer to "ma-KA-i," a three-syllable word with the last two syllables almost merging.

Hint for Longer Words: Repetition and Rhythm. Have you noticed the tendency in long Hawaiian words for groups of letters to repeat? That kind of repetition is fairly common. When you see a long Hawaiian word, don't panic. Identify its repeating letter groups, figure out how to pronounce them individually, then put the whole word together. Chances are you'll come pretty close to getting it correct.

For example, *Waianapanapa* throws a lot of people. But look at the repeating letter group napa (na-pa). See the word as "Waia/napa/napa." So, two "na-pa"s prefixed with a "wai-a" (the ai in wai merges here)—that makes "wai-a/na-pa/na-pa." Once you've identified the repeating groups, the rhythm of the word comes naturally. Try this approach for longer words, including the state fish: *humuhumunukunukuapuaa:* two "hu-mu"s, two "nu-ku"s, and an "a-pu-a-a." Now try it: "hu-mu/hu-mu/nu-ku/nu-ku/a-pu-a-a." . . . Very good!

Makai **and** *mauka.* In Hawaii, local people often give directions or describe the location of a place as makai (merge the *ai*), which means "toward the sea," or *mauka* (merge the *au*), which means "toward the mountains; inland." I had a terrible time remembering which was which until I came up with this mnemonic:

Go *makai*
Where sea meets sky,

and Tom Winnett came up with:

Mauka is toward the MAUntains.

However, I still think in terms of left, right, north, south, east, and west. I don't often use *mauka* and *makai* in this book.

Do your best, with respect. Approach the language with respect, and give it your best shot. Then be prepared to hear local people pronounce it differently. Learn from them. Maybe it's part of our jobs as visitors to inadvertently provide a little comic relief for those living and working here as opposed to just vacationing here.

Instant Hawaiian (see Bibliography) is a useful booklet that's a lot less frivolous than its title implies. It begins, "So you'd like to learn to speak Hawaiian—you should live so long!" I felt I'd come to the right place. Look for it when you get to Maui.

Geology and History, Natural and Human

First, the earth

According to the theory of *plate tectonics*, the earth consists of:

A rigid, rocky outer shell, the *lithosphere* ("rocky zone").

Beneath the lithosphere, a hot, semifluid layer, the *asthenosphere* ("weak zone").

A core that doesn't play a part in this oversimplified discussion.

The lithosphere is broken into *plates* that move with respect to one another. Hot, fluid material, possibly from the asthenosphere or melted by contact with the asthenosphere, penetrates up through the lithosphere at three kinds of places:

Mid-oceanic ridges, where plates spread apart.

Subduction zones, where plates collide and one dives under the other (subducts).

Hot spots, where a plume of molten material appears in the middle of a plate.

Next, the land

It's believed that the Hawaiian Islands exist where the Pacific Plate, on which they ride, is moving northwest across a hot spot. An undersea volcano is built at the place where the plate is over the hot spot. If the volcano gets big enough, it breaks the ocean's surface to become an island. Eventually, the plate's movement carries the island far enough away from the hot spot that volcanism ceases on that island. Erosion, which begins the moment the new island appears above the sea, tears the land down.

The Hawaiian Islands are successively older toward the northwest and younger toward the southeast. Northwestern islands, like Necker, are hardly more than bits of volcanic rock now. Southeastern islands, including the major Hawaiian Islands, are still sig-

10

nificant chunks of land. The big island of Hawaii is the youngest and the farthest southeast of the major islands; Maui is the next youngest; and Kauai and Niihau are the oldest and the farthest northwest of the major islands.

The molten material—lava—characteristic of Hawaiian volcanoes is relatively fluid. The fluidity of the lava allows it to spread widely, and repeated eruptions produce broad-based, rounded volcanoes called shield volcanoes. The volcano expels not only flowing lava but volcanic fragments such as cinder and ash. Alternating layers of these materials build up during periods of volcanic activity.

Erosion has sculpted the exotic landscapes we associate with volcanic tropical islands. Waves pound the volcano's edges, undercutting them and, where the volcano slopes more steeply, forming cliffs. Streams take material from higher on the volcano, cutting valleys into its flanks and depositing the material they carry as alluvium, like the broad alluvial apron formed on the isthmus side of West Maui by the deposits of four of its streams: Waihee, Waiehu, Iao, and Waikapu. New episodes of volcanism wholly or partly fill in those landscapes, and erosional forces immediately begin sculpting the new surface as well as the remaining older surface.

Maui is geologically an infant on an Earth more than four billion years old. Potassium-argon dating of rocks suggests that lava welled forth to build West Maui beginning a little less than two million years ago. Volcanism ended on West Maui just over a million years ago. Haleakala literally burst upon the scene less than a million years ago. Outpourings from Haleakala built the isthmus that now connects West and East Maui. West Maui's volcano, Puu Kukui, may be extinct now; East Maui—Haleakala—is only dormant. The last lava flow on Maui occurred along Haleakala's southwest rift zone in about 1790, forming Cape Kinau and dividing what had been one huge bay into Ahihi and La Pérouse bays. Haleakala may erupt again; no one knows whether it will or when or where. On West Maui, and on East Maui while Haleakala sleeps, erosion reigns, changing the landscape constantly.

Life arrives

Living organisms colonize new land rapidly. In Hawaii, plants established themselves once there was a little soil for them. Seeds arrived on the air currents, or floated in on the sea, or hitched a ride on the feathers or in the guts of birds. Insects and spiders also took advantage of the air currents. Birds were certainly among the first visitors. Living things found little competition and quickly adapted to their new home, evolving into an astonishing variety of species many of which occur naturally only on the Hawaiian islands ("endemic to Hawaii"). The only mammals to arrive were the bat and the seal. Some birds became flightless—a fairly common adaptation on isolated islands with no ground predators.

People arrive

It's unlikely that the site of the very first human colony in the Hawaiian Islands will ever be found. Too much time has passed; too many destructive forces have been at work. However, recent archaeological work has established that people had settled in Hawaii by 300–400 A.D., earlier than had previously been thought. Linguistic studies and cultural artifacts recovered from sites of early colonization point to the Marquesas Islands as the colonizers' home; the Marquesas themselves seem to have been colonized as early as 200 B.C.

The colonizers of Hawaii had to adapt the Marquesan technology to their new home. For example, the Marquesans made distinctive large, one-piece fishhooks from the large, strong pearl shells that abounded in Marquesan waters. There are no such large shells in Hawaiian waters, so the colonists developed two-piece fishhooks made of the weaker materials that were available in Hawaii (such as bone and wood). Over time, a uniquely Hawaiian material culture developed.

At one time, scholars believed that, as related in Hawaii's oral traditions and genealogies, a later wave of colonizers from Tahiti swept in and conquered the earlier Hawaiians. Research does not support that theory. Instead, research has revealed that before European contact, Hawaiian material culture evolved steadily in patterns that suggest gradual and local, not abrupt and external, influences. The archaeological record hints that there may have been some Hawaiian-Tahitian contact in the twelfth century, but its influence was slight.

The Hawaiians profoundly altered the environment of the islands. They had brought with them the plants they had found most useful in the Marquesas Islands: taro, ti , the trees from which they made a bark cloth (tapa), sugar cane, ginger, gourd plants, yams, bamboo, turmeric, arrowroot, and the breadfruit tree. They also brought the small pigs of Polynesia, dogs, jungle fowl, and, probably as stowaways, rats. They used slash-and-burn techniques to clear the native lowland forests for the crops they had brought. Habitat loss together with competition for food with and predation by the newly introduced animals wrought havoc with the native animals, particularly birds. Many species of birds had already become extinct long before Europeans arrived.

On the eve of the Europeans' accidental stumbling across Hawaii, the major Hawaiian islands held substantial numbers of people of Polynesian descent. They had no written language, but their oral and musical traditions were ancient and rich. Their social system was highly stratified and very rigid. Commoners, or makaainana, lived in self-sufficient family groups and villages, farming and fishing for most necessities and trading for necessities they could not otherwise obtain. The land was divided among hereditary chiefs of the noble class (alii). Commoners paid part of their crops or catches as taxes to the chief who ruled the land-division they lived on; commoners served their chief as soldiers. Higher chiefs ruled over lower chiefs, receiving from them taxes and also commoners to serve as soldiers. People especially gifted in healing, divination, or important crafts served the populace in those capacities (for example, as priests). There was also a class of untouchables, the kauwa. Most people were at death what they had been at birth.

Strict laws defined what was forbidden, or kapu, and governed the conduct of kauwa toward everyone else, of commoners toward alii, of alii of a lower rank toward alii of higher rank, and of men and women toward each other. Some of the laws seem irrationally harsh. For example, a commoner could be put to death if his shadow fell on an alii.

Chiefs frequently made war on one another. If the chiefs of one island were united under a high chief or a king, often that island would make war on the other islands. In the late 1700s, war raged between Maui and the big island of Hawaii for many years. Hawaii's king was able to hold Maui's Hana district for much of the time, and periodically he tried to conquer the rest of Maui. The young warrior and future king Kamehameha served Hawaii's king and first saw combat in these wars against Maui.

The Hawaiians worshipped many gods and goddesses. The principal ones were Ku, Kane, Kanaloa, and Lono. Ku represented the male aspect of the natural world. Ku was also the god of war, and he demanded human sacrifice. Kane was the god of life, a benevolent god who was regarded as the Creator and the ancestor of all Hawaiians. Kanaloa ruled the dead and the dark aspects of life, and he was often linked with Kane in worship.

Lono was another benevolent god; he ruled clouds, rain, and harvests. The annual winter festival in Lono's honor, Makahiki, ran from October to February. *Makahiki* was a time of harvest, celebration, fewer *kapu*, and sporting events. Images of Lono were carried around each island atop tall poles with crosspieces from which banners of white *tapa* flew. (Legend said Lono had sailed away from Hawaii long ago and would return in a floating *heiau* (temple) decked with poles flying long white banners from their crosspieces.) Chiefs and chiefesses met the image of Lono with ceremonies and gifts, and commoners came forward to pay their taxes.

Systems like that can last for hundreds and even thousands of years in the absence of compelling internal problems or changes and of external forces, as the Hawaiian system did. But change eventually comes.

The Europeans arrive by accident

Christopher Columbus had sailed from Spain to what he thought was the Orient, hoping to find a sea route to replace the long, hazardous land route. But in fact he discovered an obstacle called North America. With a direct sea route between Europe and the Orient blocked, people sought other sea routes. The southern routes around the Cape of Good Hope at the tip of Africa and Cape Horn at the tip of South America proved to be very long and very treacherous. Still, the trade was lucrative. The European demand for Oriental goods such as spices, Chinese porcelain, and silk was insatiable. By trading their way around the world, a captain, his crew, and the government or the tradesmen that financed them might become very wealthy in just one voyage.

All over Europe, people came to believe that a good, navigable route *must* exist in northern waters that would allow them to sail west from Europe around the northern end of North America to the Orient. (It doesn't exist.) Captain James Cook sailed from England on July 12, 1776, to try to find the Northwest Passage from the Pacific side.

In December of 1777, Cook left Tahiti sailing northeast, not expecting to see land again until he reached North America. Instead, he sighted land on January 18, 1778, and reached the southeast shore of Kauai on January 19th. In Hawaii, it was the time of *Makahiki*, the festival honoring the god Lono. The Hawaiians mistook the masts and sails of Cook's ships for the poles and tapa banners of the floating *heiau* on which Lono was to return and received Cook as if he were Lono.

Cook was an intelligent and compassionate man who respected the native societies he found and who tried to deal with their people

fairly and decently. He tried to keep crewmen who he knew had
venereal diseases from infecting the natives, but he failed. Cook did
not stay long in Hawaii. He spent most of 1778 searching for the
Northwest Passage; unsuccessful, he returned to Hawaii in early
1779 to make repairs and resupply. It was *Makahiki* again. All went
well at first, but the Hawaiians stole an auxiliary boat from one of his
ships. When he tried to retrieve it, there was a brief skirmish, in
which Cook and four of his crew were killed.

Cook's ships survived a second futile search for the Northwest
Passage, after which the crew sailed westward for England, stopping
in China. There the crew learned the astonishing value of another of
the expedition's great discoveries: the furs of the sea otters and seals
of the Pacific Northwest. Trade with the Orient suddenly became
even more profitable, and Hawaii was to become not an isolated
curiosity but an important point on a major world trade route.

In Hawaii, the young chief Kamehameha began his conquest of
the islands in 1790. Kamehameha actively sought Western allies,
weapons, and advice. He subdued Maui for the first time after a
bloody battle in Iao Valley. Maui's defiant king recaptured the island;
years passed before Kamehameha reconquered Maui. He conquered
all the islands but Kauai and Niihau.

Kamehameha's wars, Western diseases, and the sandalwood
trade decimated the native Hawaiians. Chiefs indebted themselves to
foreign merchants for weapons and other goods. New England merchants discovered that Hawaii had abundant sandalwood, for which
the Chinese would pay huge prices. Merchants demanded payment
from the chiefs in sandalwood; the chiefs ordered the commoners
into the mountains to get the precious wood. The heartwood nearest
the roots was the best part; the whole tree had to be destroyed to get
it. The mountains were stripped of their sandalwood trees. Many of
those ordered into the mountains died of exposure and starvation.
Communities that had depended on their labor for food also starved.

Kamehameha I died in 1819, leaving the monarchy to his son
Liholiho and a regency in Liholiho's behalf to his favorite wife,
Kaahumanu. Liholiho was an amiable, weak-willed alcoholic.
Kaahumanu was strong-willed, intelligent, capable, and ambitious.
She believed that the old Hawaiian *kapu* system was obsolete: no
gods struck down the Westerners, who daily did things that were
kapu for Hawaiians. Six months after Kamehameha I's death, she
persuaded Liholiho to join her in breaking several ancient *kapu*. The
kapu system, having been discredited, crumbled; the old order was
dead.

Plaque at Kaahumanu's birthplace

The missionaries arrive

Congregationalist missionaries from New England reached Hawaii in 1820; Liholiho grudgingly gave them a year's trial. The end of the *kapu* system had left a religious vacuum into which the missionaries moved remarkably easily. To their credit, they came with a sincere desire to commit their lives to bettering those of the people of Hawaii. Liholiho's mother converted to Christianity and made it acceptable for other *alii* to follow her example. Kaahumanu became a convert, too, and set about remodeling Hawaii socially and politically, based on the Ten Commandments.

An ecosystem passes

Cook and those who came after him gave cattle, goats, and large European pigs as gifts to the Hawaiian chiefs, and the animals over-ran the islands. They ate everything. Rainwater sluiced off the now-bare hillsides without replenishing the aquifers. Areas that had been blessed with an abundance of water suffered drought now. Native plants could not reestablish themselves because the unrestrained animals ate them as soon as they sent up a shoot. People wrongly concluded that native plants were inherently unable to reestablish themselves, and they imported non-native trees like the eucalyptuses and ironwoods that you see so often today.

The native habitat area and diversity shrank still more before the new sugar plantations. Planters drained wetlands for the commercially valuable crop and erected dams, ditches, and sluices to divert the natural water supply into a controllable water supply. What they did was not so very different from what the Polynesians had done when they had cleared the native lowland forests in order to plant their taro, but the scale was far vaster. In one particularly terrible mistake, growers imported the mongoose to prey on the rats that damaged their crops. But the rat forages at night, while the mongoose hunts by day: they seldom met. What the mongooses preyed on instead were the eggs of native ground-nesting birds.

Few of Hawaii's native plants put forth showy flowers or set palatable fruit, so the new settlers imported ornamental and fruiting plants to brighten their gardens and tables. Many shrubs and trees did so well in Hawaii's favorable climate that they escaped into the wild to become pest plants, crowding out native species and interrupting the food chain.

Birds brought over as pets escaped to compete with native species. More species of native birds have become extinct in Hawaii than anywhere else in the world, and most of the birds you see will be introduced species like the zebra dove and the myna.

It is tragic but true that when you visit Hawaii, you will probably see very few of its native plants and animals. The dryland forest on Haleakala's upper, western slopes and the alpine plants in Haleakala's crater, now fenced to keep out goats and pigs, offer you chances to see remnants of native Hawaiian plant communities.

A culture passes

Literacy replaced the rich Hawaiian oral tradition, and many legends and stories were forgotten before someone thought to write them down. The significance of many place names, apart from their literal meaning, has been lost forever. Zealous missionaries and converts believed that the native traditions were evil, and they nearly succeeded in eradicating all traces of the native culture.

A nation passes

Hawaiians saw that their only hope of surviving as an independent nation in the modern world was to secure the protection and guarantees of freedom of one of the major powers. The Hawaiian monarchs would have preferred the British, but British influence was ultimately inadequate to withstand American influence. American missionaries doled out God's grace. American entrepreneurs established plantations and businesses. American ships filled the harbors.

Economic and cultural domination of Hawaii eventually passed into American hands, particularly after the new land laws of 1850 made it possible for foreigners to own land in Hawaii. The Hawaiian monarchy lasted until 1893, but most of its economic and therefore its political power was gone. Hawaii as an independent nation disappeared soon after.

A race passes

The native Hawaiian people lost much of their importance in the changing, Westernized economy early in the nineteenth century. The burgeoning sugar and pineapple plantations needed laborers, and the Hawaiians were diligent, capable hired hands when they wanted to be. But they did not comprehend the idea of hiring themselves out as day laborers for wages. Planters began to import laborers from other parts of the world: China, Japan, the Philippines, Portugal. Many imported laborers stayed, married, raised families, and went on to establish their own successful businesses. The Hawaiians were soon a minority in their own land.

The numbers of full-blooded Hawaiians declined precipitously throughout the nineteenth century. Beginning with the tragic introduction of venereal disease by Cook's men, venereal diseases swept through the native population who, particularly at *Makahiki*, exchanged partners freely. Venereal disease often leaves its victims sterile, and many who had survived Western diseases, wars, and the sandalwood trade were unable to reproduce. Others married foreigners, so their children were only part Hawaiian. Today most authorities believe that there are no full-blooded Hawaiians left, not even on Niihau, the only island where Hawaiian is still the language of everyday life.

Hawaii becomes American

In the late nineteenth century, the Hawaiian monarchy seemed to some powerful businessmen and civic leaders of American descent to get in the way of the smooth conduct of business. They thought Hawaii would be better off as an American territory. Queen Liliuokalani did not agree. She wanted to assert Hawaii's independence and the authority of its monarchs. The business community plotted a coup, deposed Liliuokalani in 1893, formed a new government, and petitioned the United States for territorial status. The United States formally annexed Hawaii in 1898.

Military projects and mass travel brought mainland Americans flooding into Hawaii. Many stayed, and so the majority of people in Hawaii came to see themselves as Americans, though a minority disagreed (some still do). After many years as a territory, Hawaii became the fiftieth state in 1959.

Things to come

The huge tourist industry is both a blessing and a curse. Massive development pushes the Hawaii-born off the land to make way for hotels. Displaced Hawaiians, whatever their ethnic background, find themselves having to survive as waiters, chambermaids, clerks—in essence, as the servants of those who have displaced them. Many also fear that tourism will result in the Hawaiian paradise being paved over and lost forever; others feel that it already has been. The story of Hawaii's evolution is far from over.

Maui Historical Society Museum

The Maui Historical Society Museum is well worth a visit. It's in Hale Hoikeike, formerly known as Bailey House, at 2375-A Main Street, Wailuku, Maui, HI 96793, telephone 808-244-3326. Call to check on its hours. You can easily include a visit to the museum as part of your day of seeing Iao Valley State Park and Kepaniwai Park (see Trips W6 through W9). The house itself dates from the missionary era and is home to a good bookstore/gift shop and to exhibits of Hawaiian craftsmanship and missionary life. Missionary Edward Bailey, who lived here with his family for 45 years beginning in 1840, was also an artist whose works, on display here, record many scenes of nineteenth-century Maui life. A preserved *oo* in one of the exhibit cases offers the only chance you and I are likely to get to see that probably now-extinct native bird. The museum asks for a modest donation, currently $2.00.

Getting Around on Maui and Finding Maps to Help You

Driving

Maui has no public transportation. That leaves most of us dependent on a car, which you should arrange for well in advance of your visit. Ask for a modest vehicle in a drab color so it's inconspicuous when parked at trailheads. Get a road map of Maui in advance, perhaps from one of the national automobile clubs if you belong to one. Even better, get the excellent "Map of Maui" published by the University of Hawaii Press. It's good to be able to study the map in advance and have some notion of the island's roads before you tackle them. Some of the maps provided by tourist bureaus are so cute they're useless.

Driving conditions on Maui vary widely, and driving time can make serious inroads on your hiking time. Major roads between Wailuku and Kahului and Pukalani, Lahaina, and Kihei have stretches where the legal limit is 55 mph. However, look out for traffic jams around Lahaina, Wailuku, Kahului (particularly near the airport), and Kihei. Road construction and the periodic burning of canefields can slow traffic and even close roads. And some roads, described below, are in a class of their own.

Hana and Kipahulu. The road to Hana (Hana Highway—Highway 36, then Highway 360) has been improved to the point where everyone can take surviving the road to Hana for granted. The entire road is paved to and through Hana. The first 16 miles from Kahului and through Paia are rather easy. After it becomes Highway 360, however, it's extremely slow (10 mph recommended), winding, and narrow (often just one lane wide, where drivers going one way may have to stop for traffic going the other way). The Hana Highway is not a seacoast drive, despite its coastal location. It's a rainforest drive; one writer aptly described it as "burrowing through a tunnel of green." It may also be jammed with sightseers. The road becomes Highway 31 after Hana.

Kipahulu to Kaupo. Highway 31 gets worse beyond the Kipahulu District of Haleakala National Park, though it is currently paved at least as far as Alelele Stream except for one 3-mile stretch. However, it is so narrow and winding that signs are posted warning you to sound your horn before going around a curve. It eventually degenerates into a twisting, unpaved 4WD road with oil-pan-eating rocks (we did not make it to Kaupo from the Hana side). This stretch is subject to storm damage. Your chances of getting safely to Kaupo are said to be slightly better from the west (Ulupalakua) than from the east (Hana).

Kaupo to Ulupalakua. The road is less winding near Kaupo, but some stretches are covered with smooth beach pebbles offering poor traction. The pavement resumes for good several miles west of Kaupo, but the road remains narrow and slow until Ulupalakua (15 mph recommended). *Have a full gas tank and take extra water with you if you drive to Kaupo.* There's no gas or public source of drinking water east of Keokea and west of Hana. The Kaupo Store is reported to hardly ever be open (it looks almost defunct).

Around the north end of West Maui. The road around the north end of West Maui (Highway 30 north of Kapalua; Highway 340 north of Wailuku) is narrow and winding. Parts of it between Nakalele Point and the turnoff for Maluhia Boy Scout Camp are said to require a 4WD vehicle. I haven't driven that stretch.

Polipoli. The 10-mile road from Highway 377 to Polipoli is narrow, steep, winding, and very slow. Its last 4 miles are unpaved and vary from deep dust to protruding rocks to lumpy clay. Allow at least an hour each way just for this road.

What to leave in the car. Nothing. Never leave valuables in your car, even in a locked trunk. "Valuables" include not only jewelry, money, checks, and credit cards but things you can't readily replace: glasses, prescription medication, identification, keys, snapshots of loved ones, etc.

Hiking

Road maps are useless for hiking trails. For trail maps, I recommend the maps in this book and the United States Geological Survey (USGS) 7½' series of topographic ("topo") maps for Maui. Topos show elevation details as well as roads and trails. However, topos are not updated as often as you'd like. That's why you should use them in conjunction with the maps in this book and information from the agencies in charge of the island's hiking areas—the Division of State Parks, Maui District, and the Division of Forestry and Wildlife, Maui District (I can't recommend their map). If you do not write for these in advance, you will need to go into Wailuku to get them. See their addresses in "Getting Permits or Permission" in this book.

Maui is covered by 17 topos, as shown in the illustration below. It's also nice to have the USGS Maui County topo map. As of this writing, no one on Maui sells topos. If your mainland backpacking store does not carry the Maui topos, you can get them in person or by mail from:

> Western Distribution Branch
> U.S. Geological Survey
> Box 25286, Federal Center
> Denver, CO 80225

or

> Western Mapping Center
> U.S. Geological Survey
> 345 Middlefield Road
> Menlo Park, CA 94025

Write first for catalogs and prices. When you order the maps, enclose your check for the required amount, made out to the U.S. Geological Survey.

Or there may be a store near you that specializes in maps. Look in your telephone directory under "Maps." For example, the store where I get my topos isn't a backpacking store; it's a mining-supplies store (Allied Services, 966 N. Main St., Orange, CA 92667, 714-637-8824). Its stock of maps, including topos, puts any backpacking store in my area to shame ten times over.

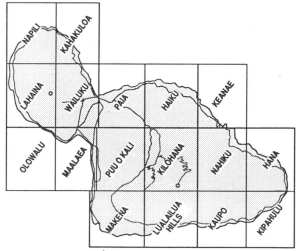

U.S.G.S. 7$\frac{1}{2}$' Topographic Maps of Maui

Getting Permits or Permission

The trip descriptions in this book include information about what permits you need (if any) and to whom you should apply for them. A few interesting dayhikes are on private property. This section gives the addresses and telephone numbers of private parties you must apply to for permission to hike in those areas. As of this writing, the government agencies—federal, state, and county—don't require you to have permits in order to *dayhike* on Maui in areas under their jurisdiction (Haleakala National Park does require permits for backpacking; see Appendix A). For completeness, this section also includes the addresses and telephone numbers of the government agencies, as you may want to write or call them for more information. Appendix A in this book gives you detailed information about camping—car camping, tent camping, and cabins—including permit requirements, fees, etc.

Waihee Valley hike (Wailuku Agribusiness)

You must get a permit in person for this hike (Trip W2) from Wailuku Agribusiness (808-244-9570). Call ahead to find out their current hours. They're in Waikapu, a community 2 miles south of Wailuku on Highway 30. As you approach Waikapu, look for Waiko Road (it's just north of the bridge over Waikapu Stream; it may be marked by a blue-and-white sign that points along it to the Waikapu Community Center). Turn east onto Waiko Road and follow it a short distance to the gates of Wailuku Agribusiness, on your left. Turn in here, park, and go into the office to apply for your permit.

Hikes to David Malo's grave and to Olowalu petroglyphs (Pioneer Mill Company)

You must get a permit in *person* from the Pioneer Mill Company (808-661-3106) in Lahaina to hike to David Malo's grave (Trip W12). Call ahead to find out their current hours. The office is in an old cream-colored building on Lahainaluna Road in Lahaina. Lahainaluna Road is easy to find because of the big sugar mill and its

23

prominent stacks on the corner of Highway 30 and Lahainaluna Road. Turn inland on Lahainaluna Road. As you drive inland toward the famous high school, the mill is on your left and the office building is on your right about 1 block farther inland. It's a good idea to call in advance in order to be sure someone will be there to type up the form and to sign it off or to ask them if they can make up your permit in advance so that you can just pick it up. The permit comes with regulations that you must follow while on their land.

The cane road you must walk up to get to the petroglyphs at Olowalu (Trip W11) is posted NO TRESPASSING by the Pioneer Mill Company. The latest information I have from the person who issues the permits for the hike to David Malo's grave is that in spite of the posting, you *don't* need a permit to walk to the petroglyphs, but you must not go any farther. I suggest you call the company and make sure that's still true.

Haleakala National Park

No permits are required to dayhike or car camp in Haleakala National Park. Backpacking in the crater, including camping or use of the cabins in the crater, requires permits; see Appendix A in this book. For more information, write or call:

Haleakala National Park
Box 369
Makawao, Maui, HI 96768
808-572-7749 (recording of general information); 808-572-9177 (recording of camping and cabin information); 808-572-9306 (park headquarters; 7:30 A.M.–4:00 P.M. Hawaii Standard Time).

Division of State Parks

No permits are required to hike in Maui's state parks, and none is big enough for or equipped for backpacking. Car camping and use of the cabins do require permits; see Appendix A in this book. For more information, write or call:

Department of Land and Natural Resources
Division of State Parks, Maui District
P.O. Box 1049
Wailuku, Maui, HI 96793
808-244-4324 (or 808-244-4354 for camping and cabin reservations)

If you need to see them in person, they are currently in Wailuku in the State Office Building at 54 High Street, on the southeast corner of Highway 30 (Honoapiilani Highway/High Street) and Main Street, just across the street from Kaahumanu Church. Their offices are on the bottom floor, and they share them with the Division of

Forestry and Wildlife. However, you should address inquiries to each separately.

Division of Forestry and Wildlife

At present there are no trails, campgrounds, or cabins under the control of the Division of Forestry and Wildlife for which you are required to have permits for hiking or camping. Surprisingly few of the many areas under this agency's control offer hiking opportunities suitable for the tourist from the mainland. Camping opportunities are almost nil (but see the notes at the ends of Trips E18 and E20). Many areas seem to be managed for hunting but not for hiking. For more information, write or call:

> Department of Land and Natural Resources
> Division of Forestry and Wildlife, Maui District
> P.O. Box 1015
> Wailuku, Maui, HI 96793
> 808-244-4352

See also the note on actually going into Wailuku to see them in person in the paragraph above.

David Malo's church

Weather

The short of it. Maui's eastern and western lobes are almost like two separate islands. Each is:

—Rainier on its north side, which boasts rainforests. Waihee Valley on West Maui is a rainforest. The Hana Highway on East Maui tunnels through a rainforest.

—Less rainy on its east side, but still rainy enough to support lush tropical growth. Iao Valley State Park on West Maui is filled with dense tropical vegetation. Hana on the east end of East Maui is famous for its frequent rain, hothouse climate, and colorful gardens.

—Driest and hottest on the south and west. These areas lie in the rain shadow of the volcano that dominates the lobe. Lahaina on the west side of West Maui averages only 17 inches of rain annually and can be fiery hot. Kihei, Wailea, and Makena lie in Haleakala's rain shadow and are not only hot and dry but frequently very windy, especially in the afternoon.

—Rainy in the mountains, especially between 5000 and 7000 feet.

The isthmus is generally dry and windy. The south and west coasts attract the most visitors, are where the resorts are located, and have the most popular beaches. The figure below summarizes the situation:

The long of it. Hawaii's weather is temperate to a degree that puts the so-called "temperate" zones of the world to shame. The humidity is moderate, too: 50 to 60%, not the sweltering horror of some other tropical lands. It is warmer in the summer and cooler in the winter, but the extremes are nothing like on the mainland.

Hawaii's mild climate is determined largely by its tropical location and also by the northeast trade winds that sweep across it. The northeast trade winds—so-called because sea captains took advantage of them on their trade routes—are dependable, steady winds that

26

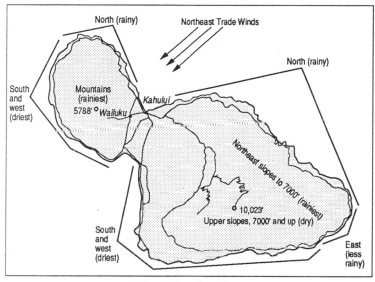

Maui Weather Map

blow from the northeast across the thousands of miles of open sea that separate the Hawaiian Islands from the continents. They are responsible for keeping the temperature and the humidity moderate. Since they are the prevailing winds in this area, the side of the island that faces them is called the "windward" side. The opposite side of the island is the opposite of windward; in nautical terms, "leeward."

Sometimes the trade winds fail and are replaced by "kona" winds coming from the south. "Kona" means "leeward," because it's the leeward side of the island that more or less faces these occasional winds. Kona winds bring hot, sticky air. Fortunately, they are rare in summer, when they would be really unpleasant, and occur mostly in winter, when the lower overall temperatures moderate their effect. Kona storms are subtropical low-pressure systems that occur in winter, move in from the south, and can cause serious damage. There is apparently no pattern to them; in some years, they do not occur at all, but in others they occur every few weeks.

On Maui, average temperatures along the coast range from highs of 79–87° F to lows of 62–70° F. The "cooler" ones are winter temperatures, the warmer ones summer. It's rainier from November through March than it is the rest of the year. Expect cooler temperatures, more wind, and considerably more rain if you are in a mountainous region (my thermometer read 40° F one clear morning in Haleakala crater).

Equipment Suggestions and Miscellaneous Hints

TAKE CARE OF THE LAND... SOMEDAY YOULL BE PART OF IT
—Sign, Big Santa Anita Canyon,
Angeles National Forest, California

This book isn't intended to teach you how to hike or backpack. If you can walk, you can hike, especially the "very easy" hikes. You can learn about backpacking in *Backpacking Basics* by Thomas Winnett and Melanie Findling (see Bibliography). Just be sure the trip you pick is within your hiking limits.

This book is intended specifically to let you know *where* you can hike on Maui, *what* to expect when you hike there, and *how* to get to the trailhead for each hike. And that, I hope, will help you decide *which* hikes to take.

This section contains suggestions which I hope will make your hikes even more pleasant, and perhaps better protect you and the environment. Of course, you're the only person who lives in your body, so you'll have to judge what's really appropriate for you. But there are a few things you might want to know before you go—things that may be very different from the hiking you've done at home on the mainland. (Maybe you already know them, but it's hard to shut me up when I think I have some good advice.)

It's up to you. No book can substitute for, or give you, five things only you can supply: physical fitness, preparedness, experience, caution, and common sense. Don't leave the trailhead without them.

Don't spread pest plants. As I mentioned in the chapter on geology and history, Hawaii has been overrun by introduced plants. It's important to try to control the spread of these plants. One thing you can do to help is to wash the soil, and with it the seeds of any pest plants, you hope, off of your shoes or boots *before you leave* a hiking area. Note also that you, like any other animal, can carry pest-plant seeds in your digestive tract and deposit them, ready to sprout, in your solid wastes. Either hold it till you get to a toilet or dig your hole deep enough to make it impossible for the seeds to sprout (one foot deep, according to a pamphlet on the subject). Pest plants include all

28

the guavas. For more information, call the Hawaii State Department of Agriculture, 808-548-7119, Weed Control Section.

Equipment for strolls and easy hikes. You don't need to make extensive preparations for a stroll along a beach or a half-mile nature trail as long as there's food, water, and shelter nearby—perhaps in your car. The things you must not go without are:

> Sunglasses
> Appropriate footwear
> Mosquito repellent ("jungle juice")
> Strong sunblock applied *before* you set out.

Your mosquito repellent should be "jungle juice"—that is, have a high percentage of DEET (diethyltoluamide). DEET is pretty vile stuff, but it works.

Equipment for moderate and strenuous hikes. Carry at least the Ten Essentials Plus One as I've adapted them from the Sierra Club. They are:

> Pack (to put these good things in; could be a large fanny pack)
> Food and water (assume that all open water sources are unsafe to drink)
> Extra clothing (always take rain gear, as it can rain any time on Maui)
> Map (and compass if you can use it)
> Flashlight with extra bulbs and batteries
> Sunglasses and strong sunblock
> Means to dig a hole 6–8 inches deep and at least 200 feet from water, in order to bury solid body wastes; tissue that you will also bury (or pack out)
> Pocket knife
> First-aid kit
> Waterproof matches and something you can keep a flame going with (such as a candle) *only when necessary to start a fire in order to save a life*
> Mosquito repellent ("jungle juice")

Equipment for backpacks. The following is a minimal checklist for backpacking equipment.

Minimal Backpacking Equipment List

Backpack	Tent	Sleeping pad
Sleeping bag	Permit	"Ten Essentials Plus
Boots	Socks	One"
Shorts or long pants	Hat	Shirts
Underwear	Personal medication	Rain gear
Cookware and clean-up stuff	Stove and fuel*	Toiletries
		Eating utensils

*You cannot take stove fuel on a plane. You must buy it at your destination.

Tennis shoes? I've noted in the hike descriptions whether tennis shoes are okay to wear or whether I think you should wear boots. I base that recommendation on the length of the hike and the difficulty of the terrain. What tennis shoes may lack that boots can provide are ankle support and soles that grip. Only you can really decide how important those are to you.

Boot care. If you're going to hike a lot, be sure your boot seams are freshly sealed and you've freshly waterproofed the entire boot, including the cloth part, if any. Use a heavy-duty waterproofing compound like a wax, and bring some of it along in order to renew the coating if necessary. Chances are your boots will get wet, especially in the winter. And they'll stay wet, because things dry slowly in the tropical humidity. It's pretty tough on the boots and, together with the abrasion of mud particles, could cause boot seams to fail.

Hiking stick. Take your hiking stick if you usually hike with one. The flight attendants can put it in the closet where they hang the carry-on suits and dresses or in the overhead compartments. Maui's terrain can be very slippery when wet, and a hiking stick can be a big help in maintaining your footing. And it can double as a spider stick (see below).

Spider stick. There are a very few overgrown trails (for example, the Tableland Trail in Iao Valley State Park) where you and some orb spiders may meet unexpectedly, head-on. You probably don't like collecting spiders with your face, but these critters make it hard not to do so. Here's one way to avoid them without killing them. Pick up and use a "spider stick"—a long, strong stick that you carefully wave up and down in front of you as you hike. You can feel the tug when the stick connects with a web. Detach the anchor strands that hold the web in your way, and lay them aside on the adjacent shrubbery. An orb spider normally rebuilds most or all of her web daily, so you've caused her only minor inconvenience. Your hiking stick can probably double as a spider stick.

Sleeping bag. It should be able to tolerate wet conditions. For example, it could have a Gore-Tex shell or it could have a synthetic fill. You are almost certain to get rained on a bit while camping.

Tent. You'll need one for protection from the rain.

Clothes while backpacking. On the one hand, it's best to go as light as possible; on the other hand, almost nothing—not even synthetics—dries overnight in Maui's damp climate under backpacking conditions. Consider which things you can stand to wear damp and which you can't stand unless they're dry. Pack just one or two of the "okay if damp" things. Pack a set of the "gotta be dry!"

things for each day plus one or more extras, just in case. (For me, it's socks.)

At the end of a soggy day of camping out. On those occasional rainy days, you may wonder how you're going to get reasonably clean without getting any wetter than you already are. The socks you've worn all day are "goners" for the time being, wet and muddy on the outside but relatively clean on the inside. While you're changing into dry clothes, turn your "used" socks inside out and mop yourself off with them.

Hypothermia? On Maui? It's possible if you go into the mountains. Remember that going higher is equivalent to going north into colder climates, and mountains are often very windy. Please be prepared as you would be for going into any mountainous region.

Biodegradable? Ha, ha, ha! The following things are popularly supposed to be biodegradable if you bury them: toilet tissue; facial tissue; sanitary napkins; tampons; disposable diapers. That must be a joke. They often last long enough for either running water to exhume them or animals to dig them up. It's actually pretty easy to carry them out if you put them in a heavy-duty self-sealing bag. (I use a couple of heavy-duty Ziploc bags, one inside the other.)

Getting hiking and backpacking food. If you are planning to backpack on Maui, consider shopping for your hiking and backpacking chow on Maui. Food prices *are* higher in Hawaii, but you have enough stuff to put in your luggage without bringing your food, too. There are several well-stocked supermarkets on the island, particularly around Kahului, Kihei, and Lahaina. I couldn't find freeze-dried chow, but there was an adequate selection of long-lasting, lightweight, quick-cooking foods.

Companions. The standard advice is: never hike alone; never camp alone.

Water. Take your own drinking water for the day. Plan on treating water while backpacking. No open source of water anywhere in the U.S. is safe to drink untreated. Treat water chemically (iodine or chlorine preparations designed for the purpose) or by boiling (1–5 minutes at a rolling boil). It now seems that filtering may be ineffective against the bacterium that causes leptospirosis (below). Backpacking opportunities on Maui are, in my opinion, limited to Haleakala crater where the drinking water supply is rain collected from the roofs of the cabins and stored in closed tanks, so that it is presumed to be safe to drink. Tap water at these campgrounds is reported to be safe to drink: Hosmer Grove Campground; Polipoli State Park; and Waianapanapa State Park. There is no safe drinking water at Kipahulu; you must treat stream water there (or, better yet, fill your jugs with clean water at Hana).

Avoiding leptospirosis. Fresh water on Maui may be contaminated with the bacterium that causes leptospirosis. A pamphlet about leptospirosis is available from the Epidemiology Branch of the Hawaii State Department of Health (on Maui, call 808-244-4288). The following summarizes some of its contents: Muddy and clear water are both suspect. The bacterium invades through broken skin or the nose, mouth, or eyes. It enters the bloodstream and infects different organs, particularly the kidneys. Precautions that would especially apply to you here are not to go into streams if you have open cuts or abrasions and not to drink (untreated) stream water. Treat water chemically or by boiling it.

If you do swim in fresh water on Maui, you should know that the incubation period of leptospirosis is 2–20 days. The onset is sudden, and the symptoms may resemble those of flu: fever, chills, sweating, severe headache, conjunctivitis (red eyes), muscle pains, weakness, vomiting, and diarrhea. You should see a physician immediately if you suspect leptospirosis. It's believed that administering certain antibiotics early in the course of the disease will shorten the disease and make symptoms less severe. The pamphlet says that most cases are mild and that people (with mild cases) recover in a week or two without treatment. However, severe leptospirosis infections may damage kidneys, liver, or heart or even cause death.

Using This Book

How This Book Organizes the Trips

Imagine the hour hand of a clock pinned to a point near the center of a rounded island. Think of it sweeping around clockwise from a 12-o'clock position that's due north. It's easy to envision the hour hand pointing to 3 o'clock (due east), 6 o'clock (due south), and 9 o'clock (due west) as it moves around.

You can think of Maui, with its two rounded lobes, as two clocks, one for the west lobe and another for the east lobe. The West Maui "clock" has its hour hand pivoted on Puu Kukui, its highest point, and its hour hand sweeps clockwise around West Maui. For convenience's sake, I'll consider the isthmus to be part of the West Maui clock. Trips on West Maui and the isthmus start at the 2 o'clock point with Waihee Ridge (Trip W1). Here's the West Maui clock:

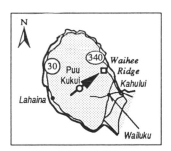

West Maui Clock

(Sometimes, the hike begins so close to the center of these tiny pictures that the imaginary pin goes right through the arrowhead of the hour hand and looks like a white dot on the arrowhead.)

The East Maui "clock" has its hour hand pivoted on a point that's about halfway up the highway to Haleakala. Trips on East Maui start just past 12 o'clock at Twin Falls (Trip E1). Distances are

33

much more compressed on the East Maui clock than they are on the West Maui clock: East Maui is much larger than West Maui, but both "clocks" need to fit into the same space for this book. Here's the East Maui clock:

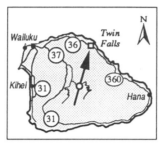

East Maui Clock

Distances are so compressed on the East Maui clock that it would be very hard to use it to show the hikes that start in and around Haleakala's crater. Yet that's the most important single hiking area on Maui! Hikes in that area are all together at the end of the book and have their own "clock" that's an enlargement of the East Maui clock area around Haleakala's crater. They are numbered H1, H2, etc., beginning with the Hosmer Grove Nature Loop (Trip H1) at 2 o'clock. Here's the Haleakala clock:

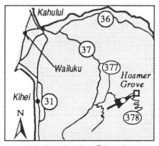

Haleakala Clock

How to Read the Trip Descriptions

The trip descriptions are in the following format, and here is what the information in each description means. Items marked "(icon)" are shown in the trips by icons (small pictures) arranged in a box at the beginning of each trip and defined below.

Title (pretty self-explanatory).

Type (icon): There are four types of trips described:

 Loop trips: You follow trails that form a closed loop; you don't retrace your steps, or you retrace them for only a proportionally short distance.

 Semiloop trips: The trip consists of a loop part and an out-and-back part.

 Out-and-back trips: This is by far the most common type of trip in this book. You follow trails to a destination and then retrace your steps to your starting point.

 Shuttle trips: You start at one trailhead and finish at another, "destination" trailhead. They are far enough apart (or walking between them is sufficiently impractical) that you need to have a car waiting for you at your "destination" trailhead or to have someone pick you up there.

Difficulty (icon): A trip's difficulty is based first on total distance and second on cumulative elevation gain and rate of gain. Let's say that the elevation gain is negligible to moderate (it's never steeper than about 500 feet/mile for any significant distance). In that case:

V   A very easy trip is 1 mile or less.
E   An easy trip is 1–2 miles.
M   A moderate trip is 2–5 miles.
S   A strenuous trip is more than 5 miles.

If the trip has a section of, say, a half-mile or more where it's steeper than 500 feet/mile, or if the trail is hard to follow, I've given it the next higher difficulty rating.

Shoes (icon): Some trips just aren't safe if you're not wearing boots which have soles that grip and which will give you some ankle support. However, only you live in your body, so you will have to be the final judge of what you can safely wear.

 Tennis shoes are okay.

 Boots recommended.

 Boots necessary, as terrain is rough.

Coastal or inland (icon): General type of area this hike is in. This is a judgement call for those hikes that include both coastal and inland segments.

 Hike is along the coast, possibly on a beach or on cliffs above the ocean. Includes hikes like E5, where you are technically on the coast but can't see it for the forest until the very end.

 Hike is inland, possibly in the hills or mountains. Includes valley hikes like W2 and E3, too.

Distance: The distance is the total distance you have to walk.

Elevation gain: This figure is the approximate cumulative elevation gain, and counts all the significant "ups" you have to walk, not just the simple elevation difference between the trailhead and the destination. It's the cumulative gain that your muscles will complain about. Some trips are *upside-down:* you go downhill on your way out to the destination, uphill on your return.

Average hiking time: This is based on my normal hiking speed, which is a blazing 2 miles/hour.

Location (icon defined in previous section): The West Maui clock, East Maui clock, or Haleakala clock illustrates the trip's general location relative to the rest of Maui.

Topos: The topo or topos listed here are the ones that cover the area you'll be hiking in on this particular trip. Topos are strictly optional for the very easy and easy trips but are strongly recommended for the other trips.

Trail map: This tells you where this book's trail map for this trip is (usually at the end of the trip or of another trip in the same area). As explained in Appendix C, the trail maps are based on the topos wherever possible. However, quite a number of trails on Maui do not appear on any official agency map or on the topos. I have approximated their routes based on field notes and sketches and labeled them "(route approximated)." Some maps are too big for one page and are continued on another page, sometimes at the end of another trip, as noted on the edges of those maps. I've allowed a little overlap between those maps to help you follow them from one page to another.

The following figure shows the trail map legend:

Highlights: This gives you an idea of what I think the best features of the trip are. Usually, it's the scenery—that's one of the principal things you came to Maui for!

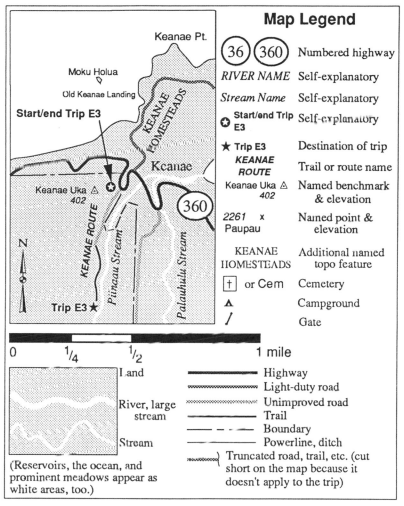

Map Legend

Keanae Pt.

(36) (360)   Numbered highway

RIVER NAME   Self-explanatory

Stream Name   Self-explanatory

○ Start/end Trip E3   Self-explanatory

★ Trip E3   Destination of trip

KEANAE ROUTE   Trail or route name

Keanae Uka △ 402   Named benchmark & elevation

2261 x
Paupau   Named point & elevation

KEANAE HOMESTEADS   Additional named topo feature

[†] or Cem   Cemetery

▲   Campground

/   Gate

Moku Holua

Old Keanae Landing

Start/end Trip E3

Keanae

Keanae Uka △ 402

360

N

Trip E3 ★

0   ¼   ½   1 mile

Land

River, large stream

Stream

(Reservoirs, the ocean, and prominent meadows appear as white areas, too.)

━━━━━━ Highway
wwwwwwww Light-duty road
xxxxxxxxxxx Unimproved road
───────── Trail
── — ── — Boundary
───────── Powerline, ditch
»oo∞o∞o∞) Truncated road, trail, etc. (cut short on the map because it doesn't apply to the trip)

Driving instructions: This gives you instructions for driving to the trailhead, usually in terms of driving from Wailuku, the county seat. You may be staying anywhere on Maui, but Wailuku is a convenient reference point. The starting point in Wailuku is the intersection of Highways 30 and 32 (High Street and Main Street, respectively). Kaahumanu Church and the State Office Building are on the south corners of that intersection, and you must go through that intersection on your way to what's likely to be your first sightseeing destination, Iao Valley State Park.

Some trips simply aren't feasible unless you're staying much nearer to them than Wailuku. Trips like that include those in the

Hana area (I recommend you stay in Hana), the Kipahulu District
(again, stay in Hana), Polipoli (stay in Polipoli), and Haleakala crater
(backpack into the crater). Those trips are treated as side trips from
the nearest place where it's practical for you to stay.

Be sure you have a good road map of Maui to supplement these
instructions.

Permit/permission required: A few trips require you to have
someone's permission to cross private land or to camp. This section
will tell you what you need permission for, if anything, and whom to
apply to. See Getting Permits or Permission in this book for
addresses.

Description. This is the detailed description of the trip as I per-
ceived it. I've tried to give you an idea of the more obvious plants and
other features you'll find, where the rough spots are, when you'll be
ascending or descending, where viewpoints are, and what you'll see
from those viewpoints. On some trips, the trail is faint to nonexistent,
and the agency in charge has attempted to mark the route by tying
tags of colored plastic ribbon to plants along the route. You navigate
by moving from tag to tag. I found route-tagging on Maui to be
largely unreliable, I'm sorry to say; don't count on tags to get you in
and out of an area. Always keep track of where you've been by map
and compass or by landmarks, as the tags can be misleading.

Supplemental information. . . . At the bottom of most of the
trips, there's some extra information about the historical significance of places you'll see along the route. Or maybe there's a story—
a myth, for example—related to the trip which I hope will add to your
enjoyment of the trip. Perhaps there'll be a bit more information
about the plants or the geology in the area. I put most of the supplemental information at the end so that it wouldn't interfere too much
with the description of the trip itself. I think safety dictates that you
give your attention first to the trip and only secondarily to the
supplemental information. That is not a problem with easy and very
easy hikes, so the supplemental information is often part of the main
description in those hikes.

Hiking table. The following table summarizes the trips and also
indicates whether the trips are backpacks or dayhikes. Some trips are
suitable for dayhikes *or* backpacks. Dayhikes listed as "ST" are
treated as *side trips* from a point that you must drive to or backpack
to and that you stay overnight at. Backpacks show, under "Backpack," the number of hiking days for the least strenuous trip. A dash
under "Dist." (which stands for "total distance") means the total distance is negligible.

HIKING TABLE

#	Name or Description	Best As Day-hike	Best As Back-pack	Type Loop	Type Semi-loop	Type Out& Back	Type Shut-tle	V	E	M	S	Dist. (miles)
W1	Waihee Ridge	x				x					x	4 1/2
W2	Waihee Valley	x				x					x	4 1/4
W3	Halekii-Pihana	x				x		x				?/5
W4	Kanaha Pond	x				x		x				—
W5	Kepaniwai Park	x		x				x				2/3
W6	Iao Nature Trail	x			x			x				1/4
W7	Needle Overlook	x				x		x				1/3
W8	Tableland	x				x					x	3 3/4
W9	Streamside	x				x				x		1 1/5
W10	Maalaea Beach	x				x				x		4
W11	Olowalu	x				x				x		1
W12	David Malo's Grave	x				x					x	4 1/2
W13	D.T. Fleming	x			x					x		1 3/4
W14	Nakalele Blowhole	x				x				x		1
E1	Twin Falls	x				x					x	2 2/3
E2	Waikamoi Ridge	x		x				x	x			1/3- 1 1/8
E3	Keanae Arboretum	x				x				x		1
E4	Puaa Kaa	x				x		x				—
E5	Ulaino Road	ST				x				x		4
E6	Caves	ST		x				x				1/5
E7	Black Sand Beach	ST				x		x				1/10
E8	King's Hwy.-North	ST				x					x	2 2/3
E9	King's Hwy.- Heiau	ST				x				x		1 1/2
E10	King's Hwy.-South	ST				x					x	5
E11	Hana Bay	ST				x				x		1
E12	Red Cinder Beach	ST				x				x		1
E13	Oheo Gulch/Pools	ST		x				x				2/3
E14	Makahiku Falls	ST				x				x		3/4
E15	Waimoku Falls	ST				x					x	4
E16	Kaupo to Bndy	x				x					x	9 1/2
E17	Fuchsia Wall	ST				x					x	3
E18	Kahua Road	ST				x					x	9
E19	Skyline Road	ST				x					x	13
E20	King's Hwy.-Kanaio	x				x					x	4
E21	Puu Olai/Beaches	x			x						x	1 1/3

HIKING TABLE (Continued)

#	Name or Description	Best As		Type				Difficulty				Dist. (miles)
		Day-hike	Back-pack	Loop	Semi-loop	Out&Back	Shut-tle	V	E	M	S	
E22	Polo Beach	x				x		x				$2/3$
E23	Kamaole Beach	x				x		x				1
H1	Hosmer Grove	x		x				x				$2/3$
H2	Supply Trail	x				x					x	$5\,1/3$
H3	Halemauu-View	x				x			x			$1\,1/2$
H4	Halemauu-Holua	x	1			x					x	8
H5	Holua-Kapalaoa	ST			x							$6\,1/4$
H6	Halemauu-Paliku		2			x					x	$20\,2/3$
H7	Paliku-Bndy	ST			x						x	8
H8	Kalahaku Overlook	x		x				x				$1/5$
H9	White Hill	x				x			x			$1/2$
H10	"Rock Garden"	x				x				x		2
H11	Ka Lua o Ka Oo	x				x					x	$4\,3/4$
H12	Sliding Sands-Kapalaoa	x	1			x					x	$12\,1/2$
H13	Kapalaoa-Holua	ST			x						x	$8\,2/3$
H14	Sliding Sands-Paliku		2			x					x	$19\,1/2$
H15	Sliding Sands-Halemauu	x	1				x				x	13
H16	Grand Crater Tour		3				x				x	20
H17	Red Hill	x		x				x				—

The Trips

Trip W1. Waihee Ridge

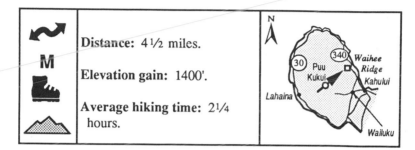

Distance: 4½ miles.

Elevation gain: 1400'.

Average hiking time: 2¼ hours.

Topos: *Wailuku* 7½.

Trail map (route approximated): At the end of this trip.

Highlights: On this route, you ascend from pasturelands to a ridge that reaches into the rainforest of the West Maui Mountains. Weather permitting, several points offer sweeping views over Waihee Valley and the isthmus, even to the western slopes of Haleakala. An early-morning start may put you at the top here before the clouds roll in.

Driving instructions: From Wailuku (intersection of High Street—Highway 30—and Main Street—Highway 32—drive 2 short blocks east on Main Street to Market Street, where you turn left (north). Market Street is a one-way street (for northbound traffic) for the next few blocks. Follow Market Street down through Old Wailuku and uphill as it becomes Highway 330 to a Y-junction with Highway 340. Bear left (northwest) on Highway 340 through Waihee town; look for the school on your left. At 6¾ miles from Wailuku and 2 miles beyond the school, you turn inland (left) through a gate onto a potholed 1-lane road to Camp Mahulia (a Boy Scout camp). Follow this road as it winds uphill for about 4/5 mile. Where the road bears right to Camp Mahulia, you should bear slightly left, off the road and up a small rise to a fence. Park near the fence, but don't block the gate. The trailhead is a few yards to the right of the gate.

Description: Squeeze through the hiker's pass-through; you may have to take your pack off to do so. Near the fence you may

41

notice some bush-sized plants with globular yellow fruit. This is the deadly poisonous apple of Sodom, not the edible guava! Ahead of you, up the slope and southwest, the trail is marked by a few small, faded red signs saying RIGHT OF WAY (or, sometimes, R/W). The pasture is private property; the trail is a public right-of-way through it. Please stick to the right-of-way.

Follow the signs southwest on an eroded track, uphill past a number of non-native plants (see below), keeping a sharp eye out for cow pies. The path presently fades into the grass, and the right of way signs peter out, too. But continue ahead and pick up the faint, grassy imprint of an old road. Where the road veers slightly to the left and forks, you take the right (lower) fork, contouring around a low, Christmas-berry-clad hill. Just as you start uphill again, look to your right (west-northwest) across Christmas berry and *kukui* trees for waterfalls plunging from the next major ridge.

At the ¼-mile marker, you enter a dense forest of guava and *kukui*. Soon you reach a locked gate, which you circumvent by scrambling down some slippery, muddy rocks to another narrow hiker's pass-through. Now you get to scramble back up to the road on some more slippery, muddy rocks on the other side. A few Norfolk pines grace the left side of the road here. Stay on the road and ignore a track that leaves the road going uphill on your left.

At a saddle the trail bears right (north-northwest) through guava and strawberry guava, emerging amid eucalyptuses just before the ½-mile marker. It's a single-track trail now, and you soon make a long switchback leg as you climb a hill. At the switchback turn, the waterfalls you saw earlier are even more visible. Ahead, there's a wonderful viewpoint overlooking the isthmus. Just past the ¾-mile marker, you have your first good view into the deep slash of Waihee Valley and into the steep gullies in its southern rim, their dark-green forest canopies slashed by the brash light green of *kukui*. (To hike in Waihee Valley, see Trip W2.)

Now you dip across a long saddle to another hiker's pass-through—the last one, thank goodness. Beyond here, a pattern emerges: you make a few switchbacks, contour across a slope for a while, then switchback again. You're soon climbing, and you may need a spider stick here. Huge land snails swim slowly across the damp trail, which is framed by ferns and by the handsome, native *ohia* tree. Look for the red *apapane* bird in this shrubbery. The trail becomes narrow, steep, and slippery here, but there's a fine panorama over West Maui's northwest coast and the isthmus.

You cross a narrow saddle just beyond the 1½-mile marker,

climb a razorback ridge, switchback up a knob, and then traverse the knob's west side through some paperbark eucalyptuses and Norfolk pines. Soon you descend slightly through tall, purple-flowered weeds and squish across a muddy track through a meadow to the next hill west. Here, you contour, climb, and switchback again, passing some mountain *naupaka* shrubs as you go. Tall sedges and branched ferns appear. *Ieie*, a vine whose leaf clusters make it look like a series of miniature palm trees, twines up dwarfed *ohia* trees, and the going is very muddy.

Just before the 2¼-mile marker, you reach a small grassy area with a picnic table. The mileage marker has its "back" to you on your left as you approach the table; it's right next to the END OF TRAIL sign. The mist is likely to have closed in here, leaving you alone in this silent, rainforest world. Pause for a rest; maybe the clouds will lift, offering you fine views. (The trail once went farther, to Lanilili hill (2568 feet), as you may have read elsewhere. But now it ends here, at about 2460 feet.)

When you're ready, return the way you came.

Bad guys in the brush. ... Non-native, invading plants you'll pass as you cross the pasture include the little "bashful plant" with its small, pink powderpuff blossoms and tiny, ferny leaves that fold shut when you stroke them. A real hiker's pest is a clover with tiny, innocent, cherry-pink blossoms and strings of tiny, not-so-innocent, sticky seeds which you will find in abundance on your boots and socks at the end of this trip. Try to pick them all off and leave them here before you drive away. Spikes of blue-flowered cayenne vervain wave amidst the grasses, too. Copses of the Christmas berry tree dot the slopes; look for its seasonal clusters of tiny red, inedible berries. Finally, you can't help but notice clumps of that aggressive invader lantana, with its brilliant pink, orange, and yellow blossoms, rough, dark green leaves, and thorny limbs. Bashing through lantana—not yet necessary on this trip—is a hiker's nightmare. Even if you succeed in making your way through it, lantana will leave bare arms and legs so scratched that they look like street maps and will leave clothing and skin covered with its strong, herbal fragrance!

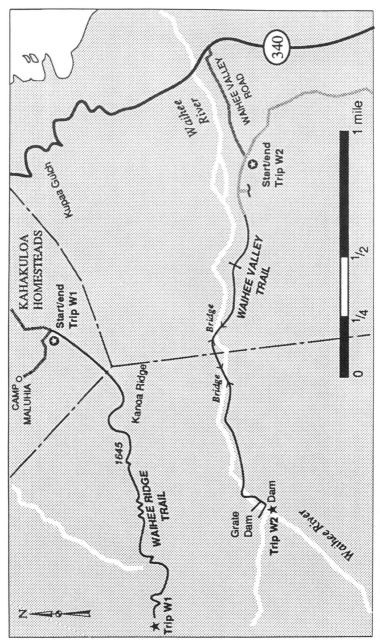

Trips W1-W2. Waihee Ridge and Waihee Valley.

Trip W2. Waihee Valley

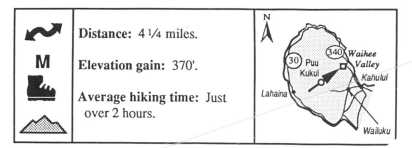

Distance: 4 1/4 miles.

M

Elevation gain: 370'.

Average hiking time: Just
over 2 hours.

Topos: *Wailuku* 7½.
Trail map (route approximated): At the end of Trip W1.
Highlights: This may be the best of the rainforest stream-valley walks on Maui. The luxuriant, exotic forest and tricky foot-bridge crossings treat you to a fine combination of beauty, novelty, and excitement. Don't forget your jungle juice and rain gear: Waihee Valley is Mosquito Central and very rainy.

Driving instructions: Follow the driving instructions of Trip W1 to Waihee town; look for the school on your left as you pass through town. Turn left (inland) onto Waihee Valley Road just over ½ mile past the school. Follow Waihee Valley Road for another ½ mile or less, but no farther than the T-junction where the pavement ends at a cane road, just over 4½ miles from Wailuku. Look for a place to park off the road; please don't block anyone's driveway. (The dirt road becomes impassable to passenger vehicles well before there's another place to park off the road safely.)

Permit/permission required: From Wailuku Agribusiness; see "Getting Permits and Permission."

Description: Walk up to the T-junction, where this trip starts. Turn right (west) and follow the road past *mao*, reeds, guavas, and Koster's curse. An irrigation ditch, mostly hidden by the shrubbery, bubbles along downhill on your right, bringing water to some taro patches. *Lilikoi* vines festoon some trees, morning-glory vines others. Ignore the side road a little beyond 1Z10 mile. Your road soon becomes very rocky and potholed; if it's rained recently, there may be huge puddles to get around. This road continues up the valley, though the topo shows it swinging south.

You cross a dry streambed and bear west-northwest uphill under *kukui* and swamp mahogany trees to a rain gauge. Here the road bears west again, and near 1Z3 mile you pass a couple of defunct cable gates. Ferns abound here, sword fern on your left, sweet fern downhill on your right.

Nearing ½ mile, you level out at an open spot; ahead, there's a steep gully filled with *kukui* trees. On your left, the irrigation ditch flows through a tunnel under Java plum and Christmas berry trees. Soon the road reaches a locked gate. Duck under the gate or swing around the posts and then follow the road northwest along the ditch. In the next ½ mile, you pass mango trees, ginger plants, and some banyan trees with spectacular roots. The road twists west and northwest, sometimes along the ditch, and always above the river, which is mostly hidden by the rainforest vegetation.

At last, near 1 mile, the rocky riverbed comes into view about 30 feet below. "Cathedral columns" of banyan roots rise on the uphill (left) side of the road. You hop across the ditch where it flows across the road and presently reach the first of Waihee Valley's swinging footbridges. Because of the way the irrigation system diverts water, the riverbed may be dry at this point. Still, who can pass up a chance to cross a bridge that's straight out of an Indiana Jones epic? Carefully climb the stairs to gain the wire-cable-and-plank bridge. You'll want to hold on tightly as you cross, because not only does the narrow tread bounce as you go, but it's noticeably tilted to one side. Watch out for frayed wire ends protruding from the cables you hold onto; they can inflict nasty cuts. Descend carefully on the other side, where there are no steps down from the bare bridge support. But there are lots of stones wrapped in leaves—offerings from travelers grateful for a safe crossing.

Bear left (southwest) into the forest on a narrow track that winds along the bank of a tributary. The next swinging bridge is just a few minutes down the trail. Over the bridge and on the other side now, you bear northwest into the forest on the path from the end of the bridge. Bamboo thickets often line one side or the other of the river along this stretch. At a T-junction at 11Z3 miles (not shown on the map), you turn left (west; uphill); the right branch is a spur trail to the river. It's worth your while to pause at open spots to look for cascades high on the lush green walls across the river.

You reach a spot where you have to ford the river—*not* dry here—on some extremely slippery boulders. Beyond the ford, you bear southwest into the forest under arches of *hau* and past riverbank bamboo thickets. You soon ford the river again near 1¾ miles, where banyans shade pools upstream and downstream. Across the river, you briefly follow a dry, very rocky streambed to a footpath that goes steeply up on your left a short way, past some elaborate tree roots, and levels out as a muddy track. The track soon climbs again to meet the dry channel of an out-of-use ditch. Under a canopy of *kukui*, the track briefly follows the ditch, crosses a streambed, and, almost abreast of a ruined shed, passes some old flow-control machinery for the ditch system. A spur trail leads right to an overlook of a low dam topped by a grate on which fallen guavas may be trapped.

As the vegetation thins, you see the Waihee River foaming along on your right. Just beyond the 2-mile point, one short, steep, downhill pitch and a few level yards bring you to the foot of a dam and to the end of the trail. There are a few spots to plop down for lunch here, and a deep pool below the dam makes a fine swimming hole. The steep concrete wall that descends from the trail to the pool has iron brackets set into it to form a ladder to help you get in and out of the pool.

When you're through with your lunch and swim, return the way you came. Ideally, you'd have views down the valley to the ocean on your way back, but the vegetation is too dense for that.

But this is the rainy side. . . . Rainwater coursing down the sides of a has volcano created streams that have cut the many canyons you see as you drive around Maui. Logic tells you that the greater volume of water falling on the rainy side of a volcano ought cut more and bigger canyons than on the dry side. Yet here on the rainy side of West Maui, there are fewer deep stream canyons than there are on the dry, leeward side of West Maui. What could account for the difference?

According to *Maui: How It Came To Be*, it's the relative hardness or softness of the lavas, not the volume of the streams, that makes the difference on West Maui. The lavas of West Maui's second period of volcanism are harder than those of its initial period of volcanism. The rainy side is covered with a veneer of those harder lavas; the dry side is not. The veneer on the rainy side resists erosion better than the softer material from the initial period, which is exposed on the dry side. That's why the rainy side of West Maui is visibly less eroded than the dry side. On the dry side, the smaller streams have eroded the softer material to create an exotic landscape of deep tropical valleys separated by narrow ridges, of broad alluvial plains, and of one magnificent beach after another—a breathtaking sight!

Trip W3. Halekii-Pihana *Heiau* State Monument

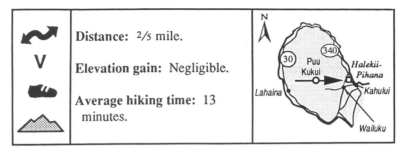

Topos: Optional: *Wailuku* 7½.

Trail map (route approximated): At the end of this trip.

Highlights: Halekii-Pihana Heiau (temple) State Monument has been overlooked by visitors, judging by its state of neglect, but it has features of geological and historical interest, as you'll see. It offers some fine views over the isthmus, too; just ignore the light-industrial areas surrounding the monument. Early in the morning on a clear day, you can see Haleakala from top to bottom from here, backlit against the eastern sky.

Driving instructions: This one's hard to find, which may be one reason it's so neglected. You can't get there directly from Wailuku, no matter what it looks like on the road map. Instead, you need to take a rather circuitous route. Follow the driving instructions of Trip W1 as far as the junction with Highway 340. Here, turn *right* onto Highway 340, back toward Wailuku and Kahului. Just as the road begins to climb a little, turn right on Kuhio Place. Go a couple of blocks to Hea Place (there's a very faded Hawaii Visitors Bureau sign on the corner), turn left onto Hea Place, and wind up the short, steep road through the gate to the parking area, 3½ miles from Wailuku. The monument is open from 7 A.M. to 7 P.M., but it's best to come early in the morning. Local people enjoy having lunch up here and socializing here later on. The parking lot can be jam-packed then!

Permit/permission required: None.

Description: An asphalt-paved trail leads south away from the parking lot, but the first feature you'll want to see is at the south end of the lot to the right of the trailhead. Look at the delicate layering pattern exposed in the low, sandy cliff face here. How fragile these thin layers are, almost crumbling into loose sand under the pressure of your gaze. What you're seeing is a cross-section of a *lithified sand dune*—that's right, a sand dune turned to stone! Much of the isthmus is covered with similar sand dunes, which generally consist of a stony crust and an unconsolidated interior (see below for more on how they formed). Many years ago, your view from here would have swept across sand dunes covered with kiawe trees instead of homes and factories. The dunes yield readily to the bulldozer's blade, as you can see in nearby construction sites.

Climb steeply but briefly on the paved path to the top of Halekii Heiau, where there's a bare cement circle for a now-missing water tank. Halekii Heiau was restored under the direction of anthropologists from the Bishop Museum in 1958. The path becomes a dirt trail now, and a few *milo* and *hala* trees dot the barren plateau. Stray to your left to look down the slope, where elaborate, chambered stone terraces descend to Iao Stream some 160 feet below. According to *Maui: How It Came To Be*, a meander of Iao Stream is gradually undercutting the hill on which these massive structures stand, and eventually they will collapse into its gully. Across an intervening gully to the southeast, you'll see a huge, triangular, stonework wall of Pihana Heiau exposed. The great boulders it's made of weigh about 3 times as much as a full-grown adult, yet they are fitted snugly together here without mortar—a work of great skill and dedication.

Follow the path south across a ridge, descending very slightly. The path, as wide as a road here, turns left (east) as you reach a ridge that connects it with the ridge Pihana Heiau is on. Look for more evidence of lithified sand dunes along here. *Koa haole* forms thickets from which your approach may flush game birds; kiawe trees spread their feathery leaves over the ruins of Pihana and fill the gully below it. In the grass around you, you'll find *mao* (a wild, native relative of cotton), Chinese violets, and a passionflower vine called love-in-a-mist. (Lacy bracts covering buds and fruits distinguish this passionflower from its larger relatives like the edible *lilikoi* and the pesky banana passionflower.)

Now the path bears left (east) and a little uphill to Pihana's simple marker. From here, you can turn left again and walk north a few more steps to the top of the triangular wall you admired from Halekii for a different view of it and for fine views of the landscape.

Return the way you came. Driving back, you'll probably notice other lithified sand dunes exposed by the road cuts. (Also when driving back, you'll need to dodge left or right to avoid the one-way segment of Market Street.)

Lithified whats? . . . Of all the things that might turn to stone, a sand dune seems one of the least likely. What are sand dunes of this size and extent doing here between two volcanoes, anyway?

The dunes rest on lava flows from Haleakala which have piled up against West Maui. And, according to *Maui: How It Came To Be*, the dunes are in a way the work of the great, far-away glaciers of the Ice Ages. Each Ice Age lowered the level of the oceans by locking water up in glaciers. The lower ocean level exposed wide, sandy beaches at the isthmus. Trade winds piled the sand over the isthmus "into long ridges, sorting it into coarse and fine layers." Plants took root on the dunes, anchoring them. Carbonic acid from the roots dissolved a constituent of the sand, calcium carbonate, which is insoluble in water. The dissolved calcium percolated through the layers, changing as it went back to calcium carbonate, which is a natural cement and which bound the sand grains together. It was this cementing process that produced the stony layers. Beneath them, as you can see, less-cemented sand now exposed to weathering has fallen away from the stony part to form pockets where new plants can grow.

The shield volcanoes of Maui, Molokai, Lanai, and Kahoolawe meet at relatively shallow depths in the sea now. It's believed that when the ocean level was lower during the Ice Ages, the four islands were joined above sea level to form an island, called Maui-nui, which would have been about half the size of the present Big Island of Hawaii. On all the islands, erosional features attributed to wave action now lie below as well as above present sea level. They're interpreted as testifying to higher as well as lower sea levels than at present—and to the power of glaciers far to the north to reshape these tropical islands.

Swinging bridge in Waihee Valley

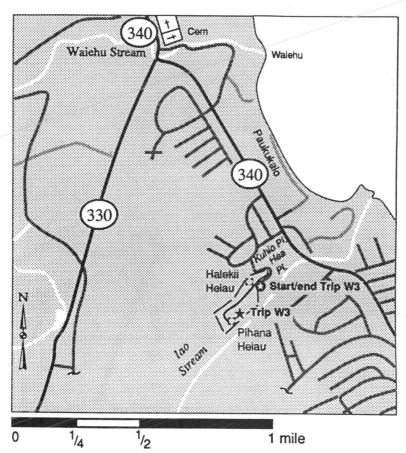

0   ¹/₄   ¹/₂   1 mile

Trip W3. Halekii-Pihana *Heiau.*

Trip W4. Kanaha Pond

Distance: Negligible.* Elevation gain: Negligible. Average hiking time: Less than 5 minutes, but you'll want to spend more time birding. *Other trips possible; see below.	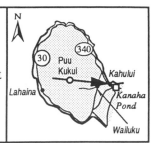

Topos: Optional: *Wailuku, Paia* 7½.

Trail map: At the end of this trip.

Highlights: Waterfowl, especially in the winter, when Kanaha Pond is home to many migratory birds. Birders will want to bring their binoculars and guides along.

Driving instructions: From Wailuku, drive east on Highway 32 past Maui Community College to the point where the main highway bears southeast (right) to become Highway 36 (the Hana Highway). Stay in the left lane here, because in a few blocks you'll bear left (east) onto Haleakala Road where a sign says this is the way to Kahului Airport. You'll be on Haleakala Road for barely a block. As you head toward the airport, you'll notice a large, fenced, undeveloped area on your left. Look for a barely visible turnoff to the left into the undeveloped area. It's hard to spot in time; if you reach the junction with Highway 380, you've gone too far, so turn around and go back. There's a small parking lot here for Kanaha Pond's observation shelter, 3⅓ miles from Wailuku.

Permit/permission required: None.

Description. Walk through the gate (be sure to close it) and out to the observation shelter, about 100 yards. The concrete benches here are not particularly comfortable, but the shelter does help conceal your presence. Ignore the occasional roar of airplane engines and the smell of jet fuel as you concentrate on watching the birds. Year-round residents include noisy, black-necked stilts (*aeo*) with red legs and in black and white plumage so formal-looking as to rival that of the "tuxedo-clad" penguin; plump, white-beaked coots (*alae ke okeo*, close relatives of the "mudhens" from whom, according to Hawaiian legend, the demigod Maui stole the secret of fire); and black-crowned night-herons (*aukuu*), the juveniles of which are brown with white streaks.

Birds are more numerous in the winter, when many migratory species winter over here. Still, a visit at any time is rewarding and educational. I watched a young night-heron stand so still for so long, not even blinking, that I decided it was a decoy stuck into the mud to attract other birds. A black-necked stilt came poke-poke-poking along through the mud almost to the motionless heron's feet—yes, that heron was a decoy—and *fwoom!* the heron snapped back to life and flapped away.

Retrace your steps to your car.

*Other Kanaha Pond trips. . . . There are other, longer trails into Kanaha Pond Wildlife Sanctuary, particularly on the airport side. However, construction activity can block public access from time to time. Call the Division of Forestry and Wildlife in Wailuku to find out which of the other trails, if any, are open. See "Getting Permits or Permission" in this book for their telephone number.

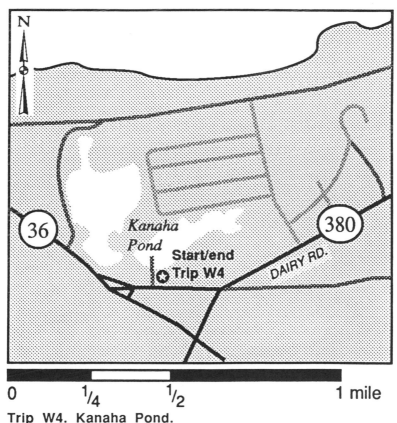

Trip W4. Kanaha Pond.

Trip W5. Kepaniwai County Park

Distance: 2/3 mile.

Elevation gain: Negligible.

Average hiking time: 20 minutes.

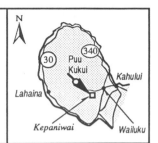

Topos: Optional: *Wailuku* 7½.
Trail map (no particular route shown, as so many are possible): At the end of this trip.

Highlights: Kepaniwai County Park, in beautiful Iao Valley, offers a unique opportunity to remember the people who immigrated to Hawaii long ago. The park also offers plenty of pavilions where you can picnic.

Driving instructions: From the intersection of Main Street (Highway 32) and High Street (Highway 30) in downtown Wailuku, drive west (toward the mountains) on Main Street, past the Maui Historical Society Museum ("Bailey House"). At a fork in the road, take the right fork slightly downhill to the turn-in (on your left) for Kepaniwai Park, just over 2 miles from downtown Wailuku.

Permit/permission required: None.

Description. The principal feature of Kepaniwai County Park is a series of "pavilions"—gardens, paths, streams, miniature homes, and monuments—in honor of the major ethnic groups that settled in Hawaii over the past 1300 years: Polynesians, people of Northern European descent (New England missionaries), Chinese, Japanese, Portuguese, and Filipinos. You can wander along the pleasant maze of walkways and waterways, across miniature bridges, and past simple replicas of typical houses as long as you wish. If you belong to a group represented here, you may wish to go to that "pavilion" first in honor of your ethnic kin; see the map following this trip.

Or you may want to try this exercise in historical imagination. Walk to each "pavilion" in turn and imagine yourself in the place of someone emigrating from that land to distant Hawaii over a hundred or more years ago. Stand near the door of the miniature house. Imagine that it's *your* home, which you are leaving forever, as far as you know. At least 2000 miles of open, wild ocean lie between you and a strange land called Hawaii. What draws you to Hawaii? Are you pulled toward Hawaii by hope for a better life, by a love of adventure, or by a commitment to saving souls? Or are you pushed toward Hawaii by hopeless conditions at home, by banishment, or by a vow to follow someone else? Friends and relatives whom you will never see or hear again call farewell to you; you try in these last few minutes to fix their faces in your memory. But the ship is ready to sail; you can wait no longer. You pick up your few belongings, take a deep breath, and walk away toward your new life. . . .

Or you may prefer simply to stroll along, appreciating this pretty little park and its monuments. You'll certainly want to spend more time here than the distance given above would suggest. When you're ready to leave, you'll probably just make a beeline for your car, as the parking lot is more or less central to the park.

Battle of Kepaniwai. . . . Life in old Hawaii was far from peaceful. In 1790, Kahekili, king of Maui, was trying to conquer Oahu as part of his plan to conquer all the islands. He had left his son Kalanikupule to rule Maui in his absence. Kahekili was well on his way to achieving his objective, but he wasn't the only ambitious chief. The chief who would ultimately succeed in ruling all the islands, Kamehameha, attacked Maui in Kahekili's absence. With the help of European guns, Kamehameha defeated Kalanikupule here at Kepaniwai. So fierce and bloody was the battle of Kepaniwai that the corpses dammed Iao Stream. Kalanikupule escaped from Kamehameha this time, fleeing up Iao Valley, over the ridge, and down to Olowalu. They would meet again.

Kahekili wrested Maui away from Kamehameha and was king of all the islands but Hawaii—for a while. He soon lost control of Kauai and Niihau. After old Kahekili died, the islands were divided between Kalanikupule and Kahekili's younger brother, Kaeo. Kalanikupule and Kaeo coveted each other's share of Kahekili's islands, and soon they were at war. Needing modern weapons, Kalanikupule enlisted the help of Americans and Europeans, including the services of two British ships. With their aid, he defeated Kaeo's forces on Oahu, killing Kaeo in the battle. Now Kalanikupule became ambitious to oust Kamehameha from the Big Island and to rule all the islands. He thought he could do so if he controlled those fine British ships and their weapons, so he murdered the ships' captains and took the crews as prisoners. Kamehameha learned of Kalanikupule's plans when the ships' crews rebelled and fled to the Big Island, and, before sailing for China, presented Kamehameha with the ships' armaments and apprised him of Kalanikupule's plots. Kamehameha pursued his rival, conquering first Maui and then

Molokai. He caught up with Kalanikupule on Oahu and defeated him
at the terrible battle of Nuuanu Pali in 1795. Kalanikupule escaped
once more and wandered in the mountains of Oahu for some months
before he was captured and sacrified to Kamehameha's war god.

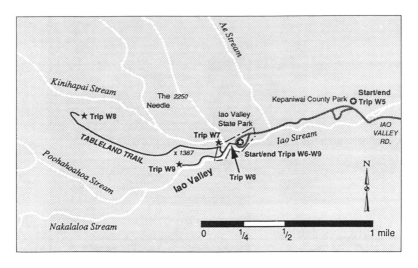

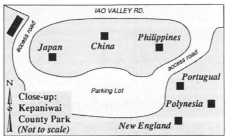

Trips W5-W9. Kepaniwai County and Iao Valley
State Parks.

Trip W6. Iao Valley State Park: Nature Trail

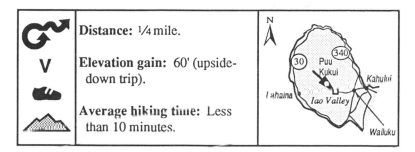

Distance: 1/4 mile.	
Elevation gain: 60' (upside-down trip).	
Average hiking time: Less than 10 minutes.	

Topos: Optional: *Wailuku* 7½.

Trail map (route approximated): At the end of Trip W5; close-up at the end of this trip. **Highlights:** This pleasant trail takes you down through handsome tropical plants to Iao Stream. As of this writing, many of the plants are identified by signs at their bases, giving you a chance to learn the names of some of the non-native landscaping plants and a few of the native plants you'll see around Maui.

Iao Valley State Park is justly famous for its great beauty and draws many visitors. Often, its parking lot overflows by midday. The park's gates are open from 7 A.M. to 7 P.M. Be there around 7 A.M. to avoid the crowds (trust me: it's worth the trouble). Whatever else you do on Maui, I hope you'll make time for Iao Valley State Park!

Driving instructions: Follow the driving instructions of Trip W5 past Kepaniwai Park (on your left) to Iao Valley State Park, 2-4/5 miles, at the end of the road.

Permit/permission required: None.

Description. From the end of the parking lot, walk west on the asphalt trail past the restrooms and drinking fountain. Trees and shrubs bordering the path include *kukui*, octopus tree, strawberry guava, and yellow ginger. Look for red and orange heliconia "blossoms" downslope on your left; the "blossoms" are actually the colorful bracts of the inconspicuous flowers. Just before you'd cross a footbridge, an asphalt path branches left (southwest), descending. Follow that path downhill past royal poinciana trees, angel's-trumpet trees, torch ginger, yellow heliconia, and many more splendid tropical plants. Some of them are sure to be in bloom while you're there, no matter when you visit! Soon you're at the loop portion of the trail (see the close-up at the end of this trip), where you wander around and through the loop as you wish. Where the loop touches the streambank, there are wonderful views along Iao Stream, especially upstream to some cascasdes.

Close the loop when you've seen enough, and retrace your steps to your car if you're "hiked out." It's certainly feasible for most people to continue to the Needle overlook (Trip W7). Sturdy, experienced, properly equipped hikers will have no trouble taking all the Iao Valley State Park hikes in this book (Trips W6 through W9) in one day or less.

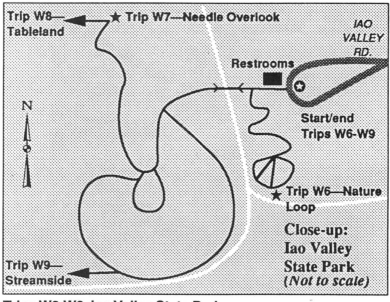

Trips W6-W9. Iao Valley State Park.

Trip W7. Iao Valley State Park—Needle Overlook

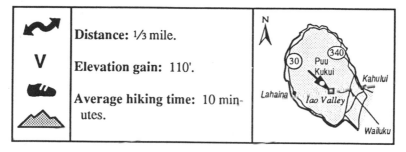

Distance: 1/3 mile.

Elevation gain: 110'.

Average hiking time: 10 minutes.

Topos: Optional: *Wailuku* 7½.

Trail map (route approximated): At the end of Trip W5.

Highlights: A close-up view of West Maui's most famous scenic attraction, Iao Needle.

Driving instructions: Follow the driving instructions of Trip W6.

Permit/permission required: None.

Description. If you're a card-carrying couch potato, you can get a pretty decent view of Iao Needle from the end of the parking lot and let it go at that. But you'll probably want to see more of it, so follow Trip W6 to the trail junction just before the footbridge. The footbridge takes you safely across a tributary of Iao Stream. The bridge offers a wonderful view of the Needle. On the other side of the stream, curve left on the paved path. (The sign you may notice pointing to the right here does not point out a trail; it's pointing out the Needle to you, as if you hadn't already figured out that that big green thing is Iao Needle.)

The path climbs slightly past *ti*, giant philodendron, guava, and plumeria, quickly reaching another junction. You bear right at this fork, pass two more forks (bear sharply right at each), and continue climbing, now on stairs, toward the overlook. The going gets steeper, and there's an opportunity partway up the stairs to stop, rest, and enjoy the view. Climbing again, you soon reach the overlook with its shelter, benches, and pavilion. What wonderful views you have from here, just over 1/10 mile from the parking lot! You can see northwest toward Iao Needle, east down Iao Valley, and south toward the steep valley walls.

Retrace your steps to your car, or head off on another Iao hike, when you're ready.

What is Iao Needle? . . . The rocky material a volcano produces isn't uniform. Its mineral composition varies from one eruption to the next, so that cooled lava from one eruption may be harder than that from another eruption of the same volcano. Sometimes the lava is deposited as a flow, becoming dense and hard when it cools. Other times, it's spewed out as ash or clinker, small particles which may consolidate with time and with pressure from overlying material into a layer that is relatively soft and easily eroded. Older volcanic material cracks as it's stressed by later geological events. Newer, fluid lavas can invade these cracks, forming "dikes" of tough rock that can actually strengthen the older material.

Iao Needle is a lump of older material from the first phase of volcanic activity of West Maui. Later eruptions strengthened what would become Iao Needle by filling its cracks with numerous, newer dikes. When streams flowing down Puu Kukui's slopes scoured out Iao Valley from the old volcano's softer material, Iao Needle and its ridge withstood the streams' cutting forces. At 2250 feet high, Iao Needle now stands over 1200 feet above the valley floor. The streams long ago deposited the softer material as alluvium at the mouth of Iao Valley or carried it out to sea. Iao Needle appears to be a spire because from the park, you see its narrow southeast edge. From most other directions, it's the last big hump on a small, steep ridge which has several other humps.

Iao Stream

Trip W8. Iao Valley State Park—Tableland Trail

Distance: 3 ¾ miles.

Elevation gain: 910'.

Average hiking time: 2 hours.

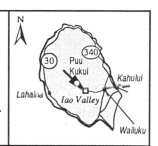

Topos: *Wailuku* 7½.

Trail map (route approximated): At the end of Trip W5.

Highlights: A pretty rainforest walk on an unmaintained trail-of-use to some good views over Iao Valley.

Driving instructions: Follow the driving instrucitons of Trip W6.

Permit/permission required: None, currently. Most of this trail is not in Iao Valley State Park. It's largely on surrounding private property belonging to Wailuku Agribusiness. The State authorities say they don't mind hikers using it if Wailuku Agribusiness doesn't mind. Wailuku Agribusiness says they don't mind hikers using it if the State authorities don't mind. And people have been hiking it for years. However, you should avoid it in rainy weather.

Description: You may have noticed, as you approached the shelter at the Needle overlook, a dirt trail heading west away from the shelter and blocked off from the paved trail by a metal railing. That dirt trail is commonly referred to as the Tableland Trail. *Caution:* The trail is unmarked, unmaintained, and exposed to steep dropoffs in some places.

To get on with your hike, carefully climb over the railing. As is typical of trails-of-use in popular areas, many tracks diverge and later converge along the route. Taking the right fork, or taking the most-used fork, is a good rule here. At first, the trail wanders uphill under Christmas berry, guava, and dense strawberry guava thickets. Soon it emerges on the north side of the ridge that separates Iao and Kinihapai streams. There's a superb Needle view at this point. Watch your footing on this damp, slippery clay; there are some steep dropoffs on the north side. Even though you're on the side of a ridge, the vegetation is so dense that views are frequently blocked. *Uluhe* fern clothes the slopes; impatiens provides an occasional colorful note along the path. Pause at gaps in the vegetation to look for cascades deep in the recesses of the steep north walls of the valley. Steep, eroded tracks branch uphill to the ridgetop; they're best ignored, as the ridgetop is quite narrow, overgrown, and slippery.

The trail presently bears into the forest as the ridge begins to flatten, and the strawberry guava thickets become extremely dense, closing off virtually all views. At 1 mile, the trail reaches a fairly large, open area—a "tableland"—of tall weeds, lantana, koa trees, and guava trees whose fruit is abundant, though not particularly sweet. Biting flies here, rather than mosquitoes, may send you pawing frantically through your pack for your jungle juice. The Needle as seen from here is just another bump on a ridge. There are splendid views of the dramatic, green-clad walls of this great stream valley in almost all directions.

Many trails-of-use lead away from this tableland. Stay on the trail you came in on. Follow it west as it passes a couple of huge, spicy-smelling swamp mahogany trees and crosses some very muddy spots. You'll want a spider stick for the hairy orange spiders who may have stretched their webs across the trail. At times, the path is hard to follow and almost disappears into the understory; at others, you're squishing through mud while ducking under guava limbs. Shampoo ginger, the low, dark green plant with the strange red flowerheads like closed pine cones, is abundant in the understory on this stretch.

Nearing 1¾ miles from the start, you cross a tiny stream (not on the topo or the book's map) twice within a hundred yards. After the second crossing, you begin climbing steeply, switchbacking and scrambling over downed wood and thrashing through tangles of uluhe fern, to a small open spot atop a ridge from which you may see several cascades to the northwest across the intervening valley. There are good views of Iao Valley all around you here.

After taking in the view, return the way you came.

Who's (or what's) that on the trail? .... Besides the true wildlife, company you may have on most trails can include other hikers, hunters and their dogs, feral animals (goats and pigs), and lost hunting dogs. Be alert for vehicles when your trail is actually a road. Many trails on Maui pass through areas where hunting is legal. (The occasional terrible stench from some unidentifiable source may be a carcass rotting in the forest.)

You'll have to use your own judgement about how to handle what you meet. Here are some things that worked for me: You should *always* stay on established routes, trails, or roads in order to avoid being mistaken for a game animal. If you meet lost hunting dogs, try what one hunter advised me: tell them firmly, "Go home." Wild goats are very alert and shy; you can't get close to them. It's possible you'll surprise wild pigs rooting along the trail. Slow your pace to give them time to get away. Give vehicles the right-of-way.

Iao Needle

Trip W9. Iao Valley State Park—Streamside Walk

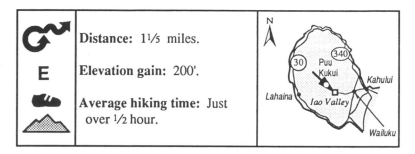

Distance: 1⅕ miles.

Elevation gain: 200'.

Average hiking time: Just over ½ hour.

Topos: Optional: *Wailuku* 7½.

Trail map (route approximated): At the end of Trip W5.

Highlights: After enjoying the overlook of Iao Needle, you descend to one of the park's streams and enjoy a pretty streamside walk through a lush tropical landscape.

Driving instructions: Follow the driving instructions of Trip W6.

Permit/permission required: None.

Description: Follow Trip W7 to the Needle overlook and then retrace your steps to the last junction you passed as you came up. Turn right at this fork and almost immediately turn right again onto a trail that leads down to the stream. Descend on this trail under Christmas berry and guava, past fragrant yellow ginger, to a lovely overlook of the stream. An unpaved path branches west (right) away from this point; turn right onto it and pass under a big mango tree. Stay on the path as it veers right into the forest where a side track (not on the book's map) branches left down to the stream. Soon you climb a little to circumvent a hedge of ginger, descend, and climb again into a forest of guava, *ti*, and papaya.

At the next fork, you go left toward the stream, descending a little, to yet another fork (not on the book's map). You stay on the path by going right. (The left fork leads to a stream view under a huge guava tree.) The path dips past an exposed dirt-and-rock face and ends at a stony "beach" in a little over ⅓ mile from the paved path. There's an idyllic view upstream here, where the water bubbles merrily down a little cascade. A needle-like formation on the canyon wall opposite you proves that while Iao Needle may be the showiest of the needle formations here, it isn't the only such feature in the park. It's a pleasant spot to relax in and enjoy your lunch or eat those guavas you picked as you walked along this path.

When you're ready, retrace your steps to the junction with the paved trail. At that junction, continue ahead (right), descending, on the paved trail past mango and *kukui* to the confluence of two of the Park's streams. Curve around to the left on the paved trail, pausing to enjoy the scenery. There are some especially photo-worthy views upstream to Iao Needle and the footbridge. However, if you are tempted to scramble out onto one of the midstream boulders for a photo of the Needle, be aware that getting out there and back can be difficult, especially if your shoes don't have soles that grip when wet. You, your camera, and that great shot may go for an unscheduled swim.

Now the trail climbs steadily up toward the footbridge and the junction with the main trail. At that junction, turn right and retrace your steps to the parking lot.

Walking upstream. . . . It's tempting to continue working your way upstream when the trail ends, but that's not a good idea. Streambanks may be unstable or nonexistent, offering no safe foot passage, so you're forced to detour into the stream itself. But streambeds and their boulders are often very slippery, so you're risking injury if you try to hike up them. You may also find the water surprisingly deep and swift. Rain can quickly swell these streams (and all Hawaiian streams) to flood proportions. If the stream begins to rise, get away from it before you're caught in a flash flood! Finally, Iao Valley State Park is quite small. You are probably trespassing if you continue upstream beyond the end of a trail in Iao Valley State Park.

Poohahoahoa Stream

Trip W10. Maalaea Beach

M

Distance: 4 miles.

Elevation gain: Negligible.

Average hiking time: 2 hours.

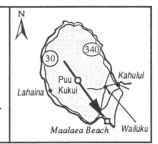

Topos: Optional: *Maalaea 7½*.

Trail map (there's no trail as such; you just follow the shoreline): At the end of this trip.

Highlights: Maalaea (locally pronounced "mah-LY-ah") Bay, sometimes called "the nursery of the humpback whales," is a prime whale-watching spot during the winter months. Its long, narrow beach is presently unbroken by buildings for 2 miles and offers great views of Kahoolawe and of West or East Maui (Haleakala), depending on the direction you're walking. Wear tennis shoes or sandals you don't mind getting wet, so you can splash in the water if the surf's calm. This is best as a morning walk. By midday, the normal strong breezes will drive sand against you with stinging force, which is why you rarely see sunbathers on Maalaea Beach. (If it's not as windy as usual, consider making this a sunset hike. Sunset over West Maui from here can be a glorious spectacle!)

Driving instructions: From Wailuku, drive south on Highway 30 for 5 miles to the junction with Highway 31, which goes southeast to Kihei. Turn left onto Highway 31 and drive about 3⅓ miles. On the left, you pass a power plant and Kealia Pond; on the right, you pass mud flats and then a narrow beach backed by *kiawe* trees. This hike starts at the southeast end of that beach, near the northernmost condominium building in Kihei. As you near that building, look on the beach side of the road for a spot where you can safely park. A sailing club uses the very last spot, right next to the condo building, so pick one a little earlier.

Permit/permission required: None.

Description: You're probably parked just a few steps from the beach. Thread your way along any of the many paths worn through the dunes and kiawe trees to the beach. Once you're at the water's edge, pause to enjoy the magnificent views and to snap a few photos.

East and West Maui are so huge as seen from here, and the isthmus so low and inconspicuous, that it's easy to imagine for a moment that East and West Maui are separate islands.

Now turn right toward West Maui (northwest) and begin your walk along this strand. There may be some abandoned junk back in the dunes, perhaps even some illegal campsites, but you can ignore them and concentrate on the beauty of this bay. Depending on the tide conditions, the beach may become so narrow at places that you'll need to walk on the stony shelves of beach rock or in the water. (If the surf is rough, stay out of the water!) The beach rock forms some lovely, clear, pale-blue tide pools, and you'll probably see people fishing here. However, the beach rock can be slippery and sharp, so keep your shoes on and watch your step.

Just beyond the 1-mile point, two parallel lines of black boulders and some old remnants of a wharf extend toward the sea from an arm of Kealia Pond. Birders may want to detour inland here, especially in winter, when many migratory birds stop at Kealia Pond. The main body of the pond lies across the highway on private property, but you may be able to spot some feathered visitors along this small arm. The mud flats on this side of the highway may have some birds, too, if they are flooded. But people use the flats as a motocross course on the weekends, so they're more likely to be uninteresting, possibly even hazardous. Back on the beach, you get over the boulders and continue your stroll until, at 2 miles, a spit of black boulders and more rusty equipment block your way. The buildings of Maalaea village rise a little beyond these boulders, so it's time to retrace your steps to your car.

Birding at the ponds. . . . Two large ponds on the isthmus provide places for migratory waterfowl to winter over and for non-migratory waterfowl to live: larger Kealia Pond here on the south side of the isthmus and smaller Kanaha Pond on the north side. Kanaha Pond (Trip W4) is open to the public, but Kealia Pond is not as of this writing (although it, too, is a bird sanctuary). I'm told that the Maui District of the Division of Forestry and Wildlife and various wildlife-protection organizations hope to purchase Kealia Pond and open the sanctuary to interested members of the public some time in the future. Kealia Pond will be a real treat, so birders may want to call the Division of Forestry and Wildlife to see what the pond's current accessibility is. I think it's too risky to stand with your binoculars on the shoulder of Highway 31 to see the birds, though.

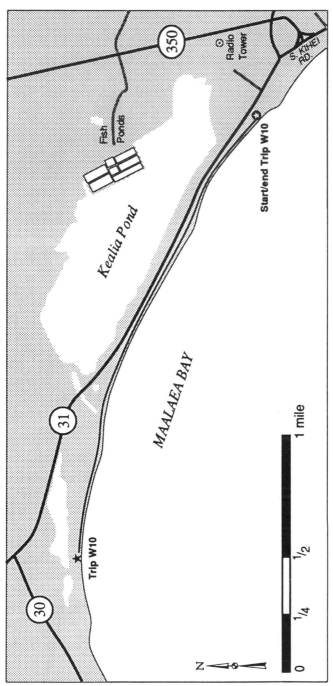

Trip W10. Maalaea Beach.

Trip W11. Olowalu: Kilea Cone Petroglyphs

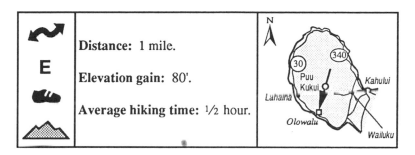

Distance: 1 mile.

Elevation gain: 80'.

Average hiking time: ½ hour.

Topos: Optional: *Olowalu* 7½.

Trail map: At the end of this trip.

Highlights: Centuries ago, Hawaiians carved drawings of people, animals, and everyday objects into exposed stone faces. Drawings in stone such as these, called petroglyphs, are typical of stone-age societies. Many petroglyph sites exist on Maui, but often they're hard to find or hard to get to. The petroglyphs on an exposed rock face of Kilea cone near Olowalu are in good condition, and you can easily see them on this little hike.

Driving instructions: From Wailuku, drive south on Highway 30. Follow it around McGregor Point to Olowalu village, 15 miles. Olowalu Store is on the inland side of the highway. Turn in here; find a place to park where you won't block any of the dirt roads and aren't taking up room in the store's and restaurant's parking lot.

Allow plenty of time for this drive—and for any other drive around to the west side of West Maui. The scenery is spectacular, and you'll want to stop often to enjoy it safely. There are also a number of beautiful public beaches where you'll find it hard to resist the temptation to picnic and swim.

Permit/permission required: None. Pioneer Mill Company owns the land behind the store, and there is a NO TRESPASSING sign. However, the person at Pioneer Mill Company who issues the permits for the hike to David Malo's grave (Trip W12) told me that it is all right for hikers to walk as far as the petroglyphs, but they must not walk any farther. You may want to reconfirm this; see Pioneer Mill Company's phone number in "Getting Permits and Permission" in this book.

Description: A good dirt road leads inland (north-northeast) away from the highway and past a house. Follow that road as it rises almost imperceptibly past an old water tower and through canefields.

The reservoir you see on the topo is invisible from the road. The irrigation ditch is usually out of sight, too, though you may hear it. The walk can be very hot on a still afternoon, so it would be better to visit the petroglyphs in the morning.

Soon you approach the west face of an old volcanic cone called Kilea 264 on the topo. Smooth, reddish rock is exposed on this face, and here the Hawaiians of long ago have chiseled drawings. Drawings of stylized human figures are particularly prominent. Unfortunately, some of the petroglyphs have been vandalized with spray paint. It appears that at one time there were stairs, railings, and possibly walkways to let you get closer to the petroglyphs; now, they've decayed into uselessness. It's not a problem, though, as you can see the petroglyphs fairly well from the road. Or, if you feel like bashing over boulders and through weeds, you can pick your way about 20 feet up toward them for a closer look. Be careful of the debris left from the stairs, railings, and walkways.

When you've had a good look at the petroglyphs and a chance to photograph them, return the way you came. (Please remember not to go any farther than the petroglyphs.)

The Olowalu massacre. . . . One of the many tragic episodes of late-eighteenth-century Hawaii took place here at quiet Olowalu village. Coincidentally, that tragedy gave Kamehameha his two most trusted European advisors, the Englishmen Isaac Davis and John Young. An American, Captain Simon Metcalfe of Boston, was the villain.

In his ship the *Eleanora*, Metcalfe sailed first to the Big Island of Hawaii. His son Thomas followed him in a smaller ship, the *Fair American*, and did not reach Hawaii until some weeks after his father. While trading on the Big Island, Simon Metcalfe caught a high chief stealing and, never one for diplomacy, struck the chief with the end of a rope. The chief vowed revenge for the insult, but Simon Metcalfe sailed off to Maui. Someone else would have to suffer the chief's vengeance.

Simon Metcalfe was trading off the coast of Maui at Honuaula in 1790 when some natives stole one of the *Eleanora*'s auxiliary boats, killing the crewman in it. Another native tried to pry the copper plating off the bottom of the ship. Metcalfe refused to trade any more. The next day, he fired on Honuaula to drive the natives away and then sent a party ashore to burn the village.

Metcalfe then heard that the boat thieves had come from Olowalu, so he sailed to Olowalu for revenge. He invited the natives there to come out to trade, and scores of natives flocked to the

Eleanora. The treacherous Metcalfe told the natives that one side of the *Eleanora* was *kapu.* That meant the natives would have to bring all their canoes up to the other side of the ship. And on that side, Metcalfe had placed all his cannons and guns, loaded not with their usual ammunition but with musket balls, nails, and scraps of metal. He waited until the canoes were within range and then fired a broadside that killed at least a hundred natives outright and wounded an estimated two hundred more—the Olowalu massacre.

In the meantime, his son Thomas had reached the Big Island in the *Fair American.* The high chief whom Simon Metcalfe had struck now took his revenge, not knowing that one of his victims was the son of the man who had insulted him. The chief and his men boarded the *Fair American,* seized its crew, and threw them overboard to drown. Only the mate, Isaac Davis, survived after having struggled for so long that the chief finally took pity on him. Kamehameha heard of the attack, chastised the chief, appropriated the *Fair American,* and put Davis under his protection.

Simon Metcalfe sailed back to the Big Island, leaving Olowalu to mourn its dead and heal its wounded. He sent the *Eleanora*'s boatswain, John Young, ashore to inquire after the *Fair American* and her crew. Kamehameha, fearing an ugly confrontation, took Young prisoner so he could not report back and put a *kapu* on the *Eleanora* so that Hawaiians could not go out to it and tell Simon Metcalfe what had happened. After days of fruitless waiting, Simon Metcalfe sailed away from Hawaii, still ignorant of his son's fate.

Kamehameha needed Europeans to help him deal with other Europeans and manage the modern weapons he'd acquired. Isaac Davis and John Young had little formal education, but each possessed a great deal of common sense and integrity. They tried to escape Kamehameha but failed; eventually, they agreed to serve him. They served him loyally and well. Their excellence accounted for much of the Hawaiian monarchy's preference for Great Britain over the United States. Both married Hawaiian women, raised families, and never returned to England. Isaac Davis died of poisoning in 1810; he had helped to foil a plot, and his death was the plotters' revenge. "Old John Young" outlived Kamehameha I by many years; his granddaughter Emma became Kamehameha IV's queen.

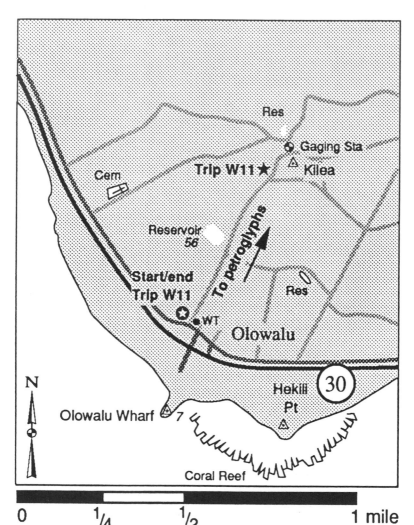

0   1/4   1/2   1 mile

Trip W11. Olowalu: Kilea Cone Petroglyphs.

Trip W12. David Malo's Grave

S	Distance: 4½ miles. Elevation gain: 2070'. Average hiking time: ? hours (allows extra time for steepness).	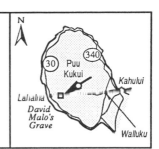

Topos: *Lahaina* 7½.

Trail map (route approximated): At the end of this trip. Choose your own route up through the maze of steep cane roads to the old cattle pen, where the "trail" part of this trip begins.

Highlights: Currently, this is the only trip that allows you to ascend the west side of West Maui. The views over Lahaina to Lanai and Molokai are stunning throughout this trip; still higher up, you can see Kahoolawe, too. It also gives you a chance to pay your respects to Hawaii's first great scholar (by European standards), David Malo. (If you don't feel up to the entire hike, consider doing part of it in order to enjoy the views.) Note that the trailhead is at Lahainaluna High School and that Lahaina can be extremely hot. To avoid the heavy school traffic and Lahaina's fierce midday heat, take this hike early on a weekend morning. Carry plenty of water and bring that insect repellent.

Driving instructions: From Wailuku, drive south on Highway 30 around McGregor Point and then northwest past Olowalu. Continue northwest on Highway 30 to Lahaina. Turn right onto Lahainaluna Road (the sugar mill, easily spotted on account of its big smokestacks, is almost on the corner of Highway 30 and Lahainaluna Road). Drive up Lahainaluna Road, passing Lahainaluna Intermediate School, and climbing as you near Lahainaluna High School. Near the top of the road, just before you'd turn into the school proper, turn right into a small parking lot for a building and a practice field, 22⅓ miles from Wailuku. Park here to begin your hike.

Permit/permission required: From Pioneer Mill Company; see "Getting Permits and Permission" in this book.

Description: You'll notice a short stairway next to the building (at the end of the parking lot). Walk up that stairway and turn right onto the road just uphill of the building. Follow this road

south for a short distance to a cane road, which you now take south-
ward. You walk at first under mango trees and along a flume; soon
you're in the canefields. David Malo's grave lies near the point
marked "Paupau VABM 2261" on the topo, above the big red "L"
you see on the face of Paupau hill (locally called Mt. Ball). However,
to get to the grave, you need to work your way southeast and uphill
through the canefields to an abandoned cattle pen, as shown on the
map at the end of this trip. Numerous cane roads crisscross these
fields, so you can alternately walk uphill on one of them until you're
good and tired (*how can they possibly get a vehicle up anything this
steep!*), then turn right onto one that contours along the face of this
hill to catch your breath, then go uphill again. . . . Stop often to turn
seaward and enjoy the superb views. Kahoolawe lies to the south.
The rounded island almost due west is Lanai, and the long island to
the northwest is Molokai. Biting flies may snack on you when you
stop, so have your jungle juice handy.

Most of the roads are bordered on both sides by sugar cane.
However, the uphill side of the uppermost road (the one just below
Paupau Ditch) is sparsely shaded by eucalyptuses and silk oaks. As
you near the old cattle pen on the uppermost road, you pass below a
couple of small tanks. Just under ⅛ mile beyond the tanks, look to
your left (uphill) for a board laid over a grate to allow you to cross
Paupau Ditch to the ruined cattle pen in a grove of eucalyptuses.
Walk through the cattle pen and pick up a steep track in the dry, red
hillside. There are actually multiple tracks; the most trodden is
generally the better choice. Tags of plastic ribbon help you find your
way up the hill northeastward through *pukiawe, ulei, aalii,* tall *ilima,
silk* oak, guava, and grasses (unlike other Maui trail tags, these tags
were fairly reliable in the fall of 1990).

The track presently bears north, contours across a bare patch,
and rises to a point somewhat above the "Paupau VABM". The path
then turns west and descends a little to a carefully cleared space
where you'll find David Malo's stone-covered grave. Students from
Lahainaluna High School come up here each year to leave a tribute
to David Malo, as dozens of plaques attest. It's interesting to walk
around and compare the plaque designs and sentiments from different years as you think about David Malo and his fears for Hawaii
(see below).

The students also come up here to tend the giant red "L," which
lies downslope of the grave via an unbelievably steep, eroded set of
tracks. Your knees will thank you if you give this little detour a miss.
The "L" looks much better from down below, near the beginning of

this hike. Up here, the curve of the hill is so precipitous that you can't see the "L" until you're on top of it. The "L" is made by outlining the red soil with white material.

When you've had your fill of the tremendous views from David Malo's grave, return the way you came.

"They will eat us up". . . . David Malo wrote in 1837 to the queen regent, Kinau, describing to her his fear that the large, technologically superior nations would soon overwhelm the little kingdom of Hawaii:

> . . . the Ships of the whitemen have come, and smart people have arrived from the Great Countries which you have never seen before, they know our people are few in number and living in a small country; they will eat us up, such has always been the case with large countries, the small ones have been gobbled up.

Malo was an exceptionally bright, sensitive, and intense young man. He was born on the big island of Hawaii in about 1793. Though he was a commoner, his ability to remember the complicated genealogies of the chiefs won him royal favor. He moved to Lahaina in the 1820s, where he attended school and quickly learned to read and write Hawaiian, even to become fairly proficient in English. He was among those chosen to be in the first class at Lahainaluna School in 1831. He became a devout Christian and a good friend of the missionaries, helping them translate the Bible into Hawaiian. He was a successful businessman, served in the Hawaiian government, and was ordained a minister. (You can still see his church, Keawalai Church, along old Makena Road.)

David Malo eloquently warned that Hawaii would lose its sovereignty to foreigners. In the absence of enough Western-educated native Hawaiians, foreigners from Western nations—*haoles*—served in Hawaii's government in many capacities. The government didn't appreciate his criticism, but Malo was too popular and too well-respected to be silenced. When dying in 1853, he asked to be buried on a hill high above Lahaina instead of in the Lahaina cemetery, for he believed that one day the haoles would covet the cemetery lands and would disturb his bones. Look down from his quiet hillside grave to the sprawling development around Lahaina. Was David Malo right?

David Malo's grave above Lahaina

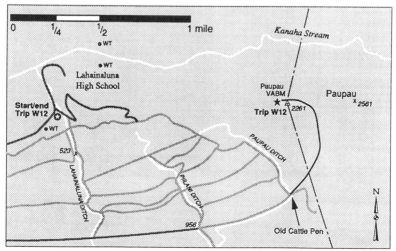

Trip W12. David Malo's Grave.

Trip W13. D. T. Fleming Beach Park to "Dragon's Teeth"

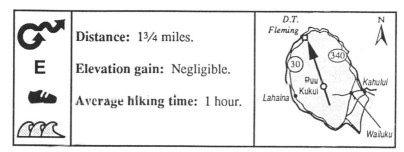

Distance: 1¾ miles.

Elevation gain: Negligible.

Average hiking time: 1 hour.

Topos: *Napili* 7½.
Trail map (route approximated): At the end of this trip.
Highlights: D. T. Fleming Beach Park is a beautiful tropical beach where you're sure to enjoy sunning and picnicking (the surf's a bit rough for swimming, and it's day use only). But the real highlight here is your walk out onto Makaluapuna Point through its unusual trachyte formations that *Maui: How It Came To Be* calls "dragon's teeth."

Driving instructions: From Wailuku, follow Highway 30 through Lahaina, Kaanapali, and Kapalua. At the north end of Kapalua, an old coast road joins Highway 30 from the southwest, coming in from the *left* side (as you're driving north on Highway 30). Turn left onto the old coast road and go southwest a very short distance to the park entrance. D. T. Fleming Beach Park is on your right (seaward) as you pass a lovely old building on your left that looks like a church but is currently serving as a preschool. The park entrance isn't well-marked as of this writing, so don't be surprised if you pass it and have to backtrack. There's a parking lot here with restrooms at its north end, 9 miles past Lahaina and 31 miles from Wailuku.

Permit/permission required: None.

Description: From the parking lot, walk past the restrooms toward the northeast end of the beach, where pretty Honokahua Stream empties into Honokahua Bay under ironwood, *kiawe*, and sisal. Now turn around to enjoy the sweeping view of Honokahua Bay and Makaluapuna Point, which is your destination. Drift back southwest along the shoreline toward the point, dabbling your feet in the water if the surf is calm. In ⅓ mile, the beach ends at the lava rocks of the point.

Carefully pick your way up onto the point, keeping outside the fence of a golf course (not shown on the map). If the tide is high, crashing surf may make this unsafe. Atop the point, you'll find a trail-of-use that leads through a wall of black boulders and through beach *naupaka*. The trail-of-use soon peters out, leaving you to pick your way across the mostly gray-white lavas of Makaluapuna Point. These light-colored lavas are characteristic of the second period of volcanism on West Maui and are poorer in iron than the basalts that originally formed West Maui's shield volcano. They're also sharp; this is no place for bare feet or sandals. Look for a low, white-flowered variety of the succulent plant *akulikuli* trailing across the rocks here.

As you continue out on the east side of the point, you'll notice that salt spray has eroded these rocks into sweeping, sharp "dragon's tooth" shapes—or are they the dragon's backbone? They're almost as tall as a person! Take some time to explore this world of gray, black, and reddish lavas, unexpected grassy flats, and small tide pools. There's a miniature natural arch, far too fragile to step on, over a tiny, deep cove whose wave-battered black lava rocks are stained pink by algae. Near the very end of the point, you'll find rusty pipes set in concrete bases. Pause to look inland. Somewhere up on that slope above Kapalua lies the vent from which these lavas poured, dividing what was once a single long bay into the two bays you see now, Honokahua (from which you just came) on the east and Oneloa on the west.

You can trace your way back on the west side of the point as far as the golf course. The sands of Oneloa Bay are inviting, but you'd have to trespass on the golf course to get there from here. So, when you're through exploring Makaluapuna Point, return to D. T. Fleming Beach Park and to your car.

Dragon's teeth at Makaluapuna Point (note person)

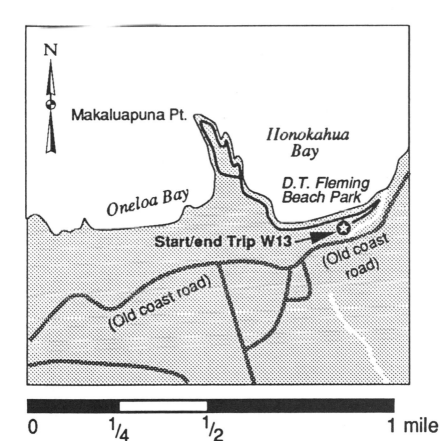

Trip W13. D.T. Fleming Beach Park to
"Dragon's Teeth."

Trip W14. Nakalele Blowhole

Distance: Just under 1 mile.

E

Elevation gain: 150' (upside-down trip).

Average hiking time: 1/2 mile.

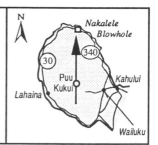

Topos: Optional: *Napili* 7½.

Trail map (route approximated): At the end of this trip.

Highlights: The blowhole is located in a small, extremely rugged cove, surrounded by fantastically sculpted formations. It's far too rough and dangerous for swimming, but it certainly is picturesque.

Driving instructions: A stretch of road reportedly suitable only for 4WD vehicles keeps you from driving north and west from Wailuku to Nakalele Point. Instead, take the long and scenic way around through Lahaina. From Wailuku, follow Highway 30 through Lahaina, Kaanapali, and Kapalua. Beyond Kapalua, the road narrows and becomes more winding, but it is paved at least as far as Nakalele Point, 37⅓ miles from Wailuku. Nakelele is currently signed; turn left into the big, bare area on the left side of the highway, and park here to start your hike.

Permit/permission required: None.

Description: An old jeep road, far too rough for driving but fine for hiking, bears east away from the parking area, descending a little as it goes. It becomes indistinct at a grassy area, but look to your right (east) for a grove of ironwood trees. Head for those trees and pick up the road again as it turns seaward to the old Nakalele beacon ("Light" on the topo), ⅓ mile.

There's no trail beyond the beacon, so you pick your way down and to your right as you face the sea, to the cove below the beacon. Small piles of rocks indicate routes others have taken, but you should use your own judgement. Be careful to avoid cutting yourself on the sharp rocks and putting your weight on fragile lava formations that could crumble beneath you. The cove with the blowhole is the next cove east, across a rocky shelf strewn with deeply eroded boulders.

There's no better way to discover the blowhole's exact location than to listen for the characteristic *WHOOOOSH!* as it erupts. Once you've found the blowhole, just under ½ mile from the parking area, pick a spot from which to watch it and to enjoy the intricate natural sculptures around this area. It's quite a show!

Return the way you came.

Fretwork weathering. . . . Wind is the principal sculptor at Nakalele Point. It's responsible for those elaborately layered and fluted formations around you as you sit watching the blowhole. But other agents are at work, too. Look closely at the faces of the boulders nearby. You'll probably notice on some of their faces a particularly lovely form of weathering: slender partitions of rock separating little hollows, all forming an intricate fretwork. According to *Maui: How It Came To Be*, this elegant "fretwork weathering" is the result of salt spray and of organisms that adhere to the rock, slowly dissolving it away as they grow. Their patient work has left us these treasures of lace in stone.

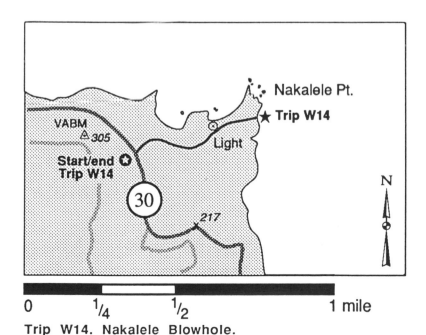

Trip W14. Nakalele Blowhole.

Trip E1. Twin Falls

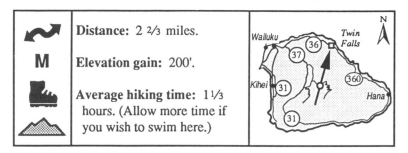

	Distance: 2 2/3 miles.
M	Elevation gain: 200'.
	Average hiking time: 1 1/3 hours. (Allow more time if you wish to swim here.)

Topos: Optional: *Haiku* 7½.

Trail map (route approximated): At the end of this trip.

Highlights: A visit to a pair of pretty little waterfalls, with an opportunity to swim in the pools at their bases. They're the first readily accessible waterfalls on the Hana Highway, so you're sure to have plenty of company here!

Driving instructions: From Wailuku, drive east on Highway 32, bearing southeast as it becomes Highway 36 (the Hana Highway). Continue on Highway 36 past the junction with Highway 37 and through Paia. Highway 36 becomes narrow, winding Highway 360 (still the Hana Highway) some 21½ miles from Wailuku, and all the highway mileage markers are reset to zero at that point. Just past the 2-mile marker on Highway *360*, 23½ miles from Wailuku, you approach the white bridge over Hoolawa Stream (the bridge as of this writing is marked olawa). There are usually lots of cars parked around this bridge, as Twin Falls is very popular. Park safely off the road and walk to the trailhead. If you stand on the bridge facing inland, the trailhead will be several yards to your right (northwest) on the inland side, where a stile will help you climb over the fence and down to the trail.

Permit/permission required: None.

Description: Climb over the fence using the stile. The "Twin Falls" from which the area gets its name is reported to be just downstream of the bridge on a trail-of-use. This trip, however, heads upstream to follow the trail as it swings southwest through grasses, guava, bashful plant, sword fern, acacia, and Java plum. Occasional trails-of-use not shown on the book's map lead off left and downhill to Hoolawa Stream to swimming holes you may want to check out. The trail presently dips into the trees, crosses a stream (possibly overflow from the ditch; not shown on the book's map), and curves left toward a fern-covered slope. Before it reaches the slope, however, it turns south. You reach a junction where you take the righthand fork southwest to an irrigation ditch and then curve left to parallel the ditch. At the next junction, where a fork branches right to a gate near which a keep-out sign is posted, you continue east alongside the ditch. Above you on the right, there's a hill on whose sides grow some splendid *hala* trees and whose broad top is crowned with a eucalyptus forest. A concrete support for a weir soon blocks your way, so you carefully climb over it or circumvent it by wading around it. On the other side of the weir, you wade right through a stream that's a tributary of the ditch, to the pool below the first waterfall. This large pool and its lovely cascade are overhung by ferns and shaded by *kukui* trees, just over 1 mile from the trailhead.

When you've enjoyed your swim at this pool, look for a trail-of-use that winds very steeply up the side of the eucalyptus-crowned hill, just to the right of the point where the stream empties from this pool. You'll need to carefully test your footholds and handholds on this short but steep ascent. The trail-of-use forks at the top of the hill. The left fork turns back toward the edge of the hill to the stream. You take the right fork northwest into the forest to meet an old jeep road, which soon forks. The right fork leads a few steps to the other side of the locked gate you saw earlier by the keep-out sign (which you can't see from here). You take the left fork to the second waterfall. It bears westward and descends to yet another irrigation ditch, where there are planks laid across the ditch to cross on (test them first). When you've crossed, continue along this ditch and over another weir (fortunately smaller than the first one) to the second waterfall, 1⅓ miles from the trailhead.

After a swim or a snack here, return the way you came.

Hikes along the Hana Highway. . . . The trip to Hana is much more enjoyable if you spend at least one night in Hana town itself (there are budget accommodations in Hana; see footnote 2 to the "Introduction"). This makes it possible for you to drive slowly, stop often, enjoy the sights, and take one or two of these hikes as you go. Trips E1 through E4 are described in terms of driving from Wailuku toward Hana because it makes sense to take those trips in conjunction with your drive to or from Hana town. However, you really need to stay in Hana town in order to have the time to enjoy most of the trips between Trip E5 and Trip E15. Those trips are described as "side trips from Hana town" for that reason.

Yes, you *can* drive from Wailuku to Hana and back in one long day, but about all you'll have time for is driving, driving, driving!

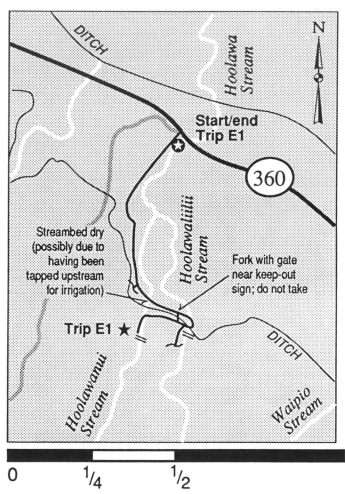

Trip E1. Twin Falls.

Trip E2. Waikamoi Ridge

Distance: 1/3 to 11/8 miles.	
Elevation gain: 100' to 205'.	
Average hiking time: 11 minutes to 1/2 hour.	

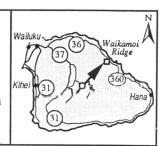

Topos: Optional: *Keanae* 7½.

Trail map (route approximated): At the end of this trip.

Highlights: The Waikamoi Ridge Trail with its two picnic shelters offers you an opportunity to hike without special permission into the rainforest that the Hana Highway "burrows" through. At one time, many of the plants along this trail were identified by signs that are now gone. However, the Division of Forestry and Wildlife hopes to restore the signs soon. Mosquitoes abound here; be sure to bring your jungle juice.

Driving instructions: Follow the driving directions of Trip E1 past Hoolawa Stream (Twin Falls). Continue east on Highway 360 to a large turnout just below a ridge on the inland side of the highway, between the 9-mile and 10-mile markers (29¼ miles from Wailuku). Park here. The trailhead is currently unmarked; if you were driving toward Hana and just nosed straight into this turnout, your car is probably pointing at the low bank which the trail initially ascends.

Permit/permission required: None.

Description: The Waikamoi Ridge Trail is a pair of nested loops, and you could start your hike in either direction. This description starts at what I think is the more obvious spot, where the trail leaves the parking area going uphill and east on a low bank. You reach a picnic shelter almost immediately, then follow the trail's left fork at the junction just beyond the shelter. You descend a little through huge eucalyptus trees wreathed in giant philodendrons (believe it or not, the philodendrons are just escaped houseplants). Look for the vivid red bracts of lobster-claw heliconia to your right. *Hala*, guava, white ginger, and *ti* line your path here.

Now the trail begins to climb, and you soon reach a junction where the left fork is a spur trail that leads about 10 yards to a concrete bench overlooking the bamboo-clad ridge across from you. (The spur trails aren't on the book's map.) There's a view of the coast to your left here. Back on the main trail, you pass sword fern and sweet fern under *hala* and eucalyptus as, 1Z5 mile from the start, the trail begins to level out. A few more steps bring you to a second bench, and the trail soon forks again. You have a choice of making a shorter or a longer loop hike from this fork, as described below.

The *shorter loop* takes the righthand fork just beyond the second bench. You descend through dense forest past a sign that says QUIET TREES AT WORK, pass the junction with the trail to the picnic shelter, and shortly reach yet another junction (not shown on the book's map). The right fork takes you back to the parking lot in just over ⅓ mile from your start (the left fork is a dead end).

The longer loop takes the lefthand fork just beyond the second bench and climbs a little past strawberry guava. This section is overgrown, narrow, and slippery, and it has a steep dropoff on the right side. Nearing the ⅓-mile point, the trail levels out, makes a switchback, and climbs a little to a spur trail that goes a few yards to a third bench (the view from this bench is currently obscured by dense vegetation). To the right, the main trail goes through bamboo to a junction with an old jeep road. Turn left onto the jeep road to reach the upper picnic shelter, ½ mile from your start. The shelter itself sits under big mango trees, but someone has planted a row of orna-

Cascade on Keanae Arboretum Stream

mental cypresses across the road, adding a Mediterranean touch. After a rest and a snack here, retrace your steps back down the jeep road past the junction with the trail you came up on. To make a loop of it, you follow the jeep road downhill (north-northeast) past two more junctions with abandoned jeep roads and past some abandoned machinery, under a cover of bamboo, *kukui*, guava, *koa*, and African tulip trees. A locked gate and barbed wire at the end of the road keep you from going directly to the parking area. Circumvent them by bearing to your right (southeast) on a footpath which takes you to the parking area in a few steps.

Hikers who've taken the longer loop will probably want to double around to pick up the shorter loop, too, for a total hike of 1⅛ miles.

Along the Hana Highway. . . . the "welcome mat" is seldom out for hikers. The East Maui Irrigation Company owns much of the land along the Hana Highway, and the company does not permit casual hiking on its land. This makes the Waikamoi Ridge Trail especially valuable as an opportunity to explore this rainforest!

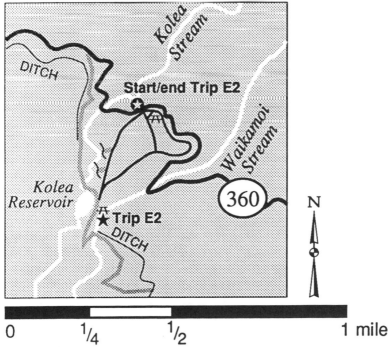

Trip E2. Waikamoi Ridge.

Trip E3. Keanae Arboretum

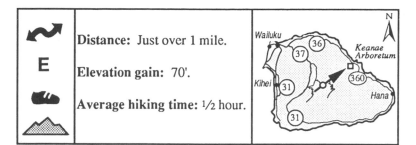

Topos: Optional: *Keanae* 7½.

Trail map (route approximated): At the end of this trip.

Highlights: Keanae Arboretum is a lovely tropical-valley walk you won't want to miss. There's an area of non-native tropical plants, including many ornamental plants you've probably seen but have not been able to identify. There's also an area of native plants, probably including ones you'd hoped to see in the wild but couldn't find or identify. Here, native and non-native plants are identified for you; what an opportunity to learn!

Driving instructions: Following the driving instructions of Trip E2 past Waikamoi Ridge. Continue east on Highway 360 past Kaumahina State Wayside, where you may want to stop to use the restrooms and to walk up the concrete path to enjoy some good views of the Keanae Peninsula. Around 6 miles past Kaumahina, look for a wide turnout on the inland side of the highway where a fence with a gate marks the boundary of Keanae Arboretum, 35½ miles from Wailuku. Park in this turnout or in another one across the highway.

Permit/permission required: None.

Description: Your hike starts at the gate, through which you pass to walk down an old road under a cover of *hau*, African tulip, and guava. Impatiens blossoms provide vivid spots of white, lipstick pink, and magenta under the dense tree cover. The road curves left to another gate, marking the start of the non-native plant section. Huge clumps of bamboo rise on your left, exotic palm trees on your right. Short side trails branching down to a stream invite you to explore plantings of heliconia, ginger, and other exotics.

A little before the ¼-mile point, you reach the native plant section. Many varieties of hibiscus are represented here, but I was especially delighted to find a delicately fragrant, white-flowered hibiscus native to the Waimea Canyon region of Kauai. Look for breadfruit trees along the road. You may wonder about their huge, round, pale-green fruits or recall their historical connection to the infamous Bounty and Captain Bligh. But surely their most arresting feature is their immense, glossy, deeply lobed leaves.

A feature for which Keanae Arboretum is especially well-known is just ahead of you on this ti-lined avenue: many plantings of different kinds of dryland and wetland taro, the latter waving its elongated heart-shaped leaves over a series of gleaming ponds. The rocky road becomes a raised, rocky path as you skirt the taro patches.

Beyond the taro patches, you can follow the path, now a rough and muddy track, upstream past fragrant ginger to a spot where a little cascade spills into a pool shaded by guava and *kukui*. The track becomes little more than a slippery, muddy scramble over tangled roots after this pool, so this is a good place to turn around and return to your car, just over ½ mile from your start.

Breadfruit and taro. . . . The early Polynesian settlers brought with them to Hawaii a variety of breadfruit (*ulu*) that can be reproduced only from cuttings or shoots (it doesn't produce seeds, though many other varieties do). With only this one variety of bread-fruit available in Hawaii, breadfruit was a seasonal rather than a year-round crop. Taro, of which the Hawaiians had many varieties, was a year-round crop in Hawaii, different varieties maturing at dif-ferent times of the year. In Hawaii, taro became the staple starch. Elsewhere in the Pacific, there were many varieties of breadfruit, bearing fruit at different times of the year, so breadfruit became the staple starch.

Both cooked breadfruit and *poi*, the edible paste made from taro roots, seem to be foods you have to grow up with in order to enjoy. Try a bag of taro chips (sold alongside potato chips in most Hawaiian

White hibiscus

markets) even if you can't bring yourself to try *poi*. The chips will
grow on you quickly. Don't think about calories as you stare into the
empty bag, wondering how they disappeared so fast. Think instead of
how you've made a sincere effort to *enjoy* taro; unlike most who try
poi for the first time, you've probably succeeded!

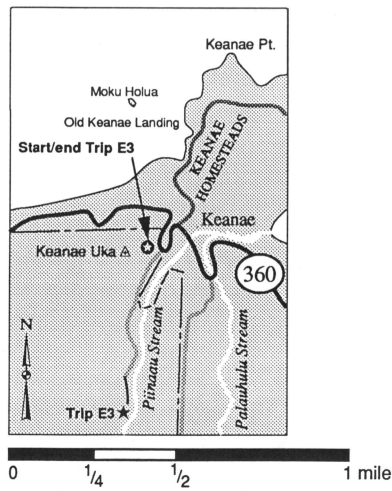

Trip E3. Keanae Arboretum.

Trip E4. Puaa Kaa

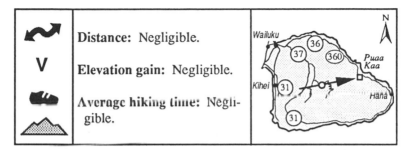

	Distance: Negligible.
	Elevation gain: Negligible.
	Average hiking time: Negligible.

Topos: Optional: *Nahiku* 7½.

Trail map (route approximated): At the end of this trip.

Highlights: Two freshwater pools you can swim in, connected by a small cascade, and three picnic shelters, all in less than 2 minutes' walk from the highway, should tempt you to stay a while at Puaa Kaa. Puaa Kaa gets lots of visitors, but don't let that put you off.

Driving instructions: Follow the driving instructions of Trip E3 past Keanae Arboretum for 2¼ more miles to the parking lot for Puaa Kaa. The parking lot is on the seaward side of the highway, 41¾ miles from Wailuku. The pools and picnic shelters are just across the highway from the parking lot.

Permit/permission required: None.

Description: The stream whose bridge you crossed just before you turned into the parking lot at Puaa Kaa divides Puaa Kaa into two sections: a southeast one with access from the southeast side of the stream to two picnic shelters and the upper pool, and a northwest one offering access from the northwest side of the stream to the lower pool and a third picnic shelter.

For the southeast section, you walk up a short rise through strawberry guavas to the first of two small picnic shelters. One picnic shelter is a few steps away, as is the upper pool. You can carefully pick your way across the stream to the other picnic shelter, which is on its west side. (As of this writing, it's easier to get to the west side of the upper pool area from the southeast section.)

There's no easy way from the southeast section to the lower pool, so it's better to return to the highway, cross the bridge, and get to the lower pool by taking the footpath on the northwest side of the bridge.

After your picnic and swim, retrace your steps to your car.

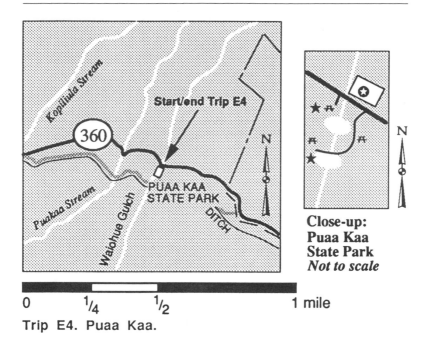

**Close-up:
Puaa Kaa
State Park**
Not to scale

0   1/4   1/2   1 mile

Trip E4. Puaa Kaa.

Puaa Kaa cascade

Trip E5. Ulaino Road
Side Trip from Hana

Distance: 4 miles.

M

Elevation gain: 150' (upside-down trip).

Average hiking time: 2 hours.

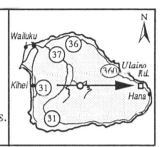

Topos: *Hana* 7½.

Trail map: At the end of this trip.

Highlights: The forest that lines this lovely old road includes many exotic flowering species, making it more colorful than other rainforest paths. At the end of the road, there's a cobblestone "beach" and fine coastal scenery. I'll give you some hints about the final highlight but leave you to discover it fully. The road part of this trip is suitable for travel by mountain bicycle as well as by Ankle Express.

Driving instructions: As I said earlier, I believe that most of the hikes in and around Hana town cannot be enjoyed in conjunction with a one-day trip to and from Hana, so plan to stay in Hana town. This is the first of several such hikes in this book—the side trips from Hana town. I'll give their driving instructions in terms of a reference point in Hana town: Hana Beach County Park, just seaward of the intersection of Ua Kea Road and Keawa Place in Hana. But first, you need to get to Hana town. . . .

To get to Hana town and Hana Beach County Park. It's 54 miles from Wailuku to Hana town. To get to Hana Beach County Park, stay on Highway 360 past Puaa Kaa and the turnoffs to Hana Airport and Waianapanapa State Park. The highway forks just past the Hana Medical Center; the left fork is Ua Kea Road. Bear left on it and drive past the Hana Cultural Center to meet Keawa Place just where you can look left down to Hana Bay and Hana Beach County Park. Turn left and drive a short block down to the parking lot for the park. It's a convenient place to stop, relax, enjoy the view, and orient yourself to Hana town. When you've got your bearings, drive to wherever you're staying in Hana, note the distance, and adjust the driving distances given in this trip and Trips E6 through E15 accordingly. You

probably won't need to drive at all to get to the start of Trips E11 and
E12.

To get to the start of this side trip. From Hana Beach County
Park, drive back on Ua Kea Road north past the Hana Medical
Center, then north and west past the turnoffs to Waianapanapa State
Park and Hana Airport. One mile west of the turnoff to Waiana-
panapa State Park, turn right (seaward) onto Ulaino Road. A sign on
the highway directs you to Kahanu Gardens, which is down Ulaino
Road. Drive down Ulaino Road to the end of the pavement, ¾ mile
from the highway and 4¼ miles from Hana Beach County Park.
Park off the road here where you won't block gates or driveways.
(Yes, you *could* drive down Ulaino Road. But it is so delightful to
walk on, and it soon becomes so rough and potholed, that you'll want
to start your hike here.)

Permit/permission required: None.

Description: Be *alert* when walking on a road! In general, I
recommend that when you are walking on a road, you assume that
anyone operating a vehicle on that road is deaf, blind, and insane.

Follow the road generally northwest, initially along open pastures bordered by guava and *kukui*. In the deep grass bordering the
road, you're likely to see the small, orange-y flowers of an upright
ilima, the blue spikes of cayenne vervain, and the pink-and-orange
flowerheads of lantana. Planes from nearby Hana Airport buzz overhead occasionally. As you near the ½-mile point, a row of tall *hau*
trees brackets a cattle guard. You cross the cattle guard and soon ford
a stream under huge mango trees just before reaching the gate of
Kahanu Gardens (on your right, seaward). Look for dwarf poinciana
trees, stunning in their brilliant red-and-yellow blossoms, across the
road from the gate.

A little beyond ¾ mile, Ulaino Road passes through a magnificent forest of *kukui* and *hala* trees, punctuated by an occasional
mango tree There is a lush understory of ferns, and ephiphytic ferns
grow high in the trees. As the forest opens up around 1¾ miles, you
pass some homes and ford a charming stream with several small
cascades. The yards around the homes present a colorful display of
ornamental ginger, variegated *ti*, heliconia, impatiens, and many
other exotic plants. The road forks at a planting of the very sym-
metical Norfolk pine; take the left fork here.

Almost 2 miles from your start, the road dips down to a stream
that's pooled behind a cobblestone barrier near its mouth. Across the
pool, a cliff of black rock forms a wall almost hidden in the rich green
of overhanging *kukui* trees. Deep in amongst the leaves you may
glimpse seep springs feeding the pool. Turn seaward on a muddy

track that leads to the boulder beach and the cobblestone barrier across the stream's mouth. The black lavas of the coastal cliffs, the intense blue of the turbulent sea, the mirror-like pool, and the vivid green of the coastal rainforest make an unforgettable picture.

Standing near the cobblestone barrier across the stream's mouth, look northwest across the stream and up the coast about 200 yards for the final highlight of this hike. Do you see it—the water falling over the cliff and down to the rocky beach? If tide and surf permit, you can pick your way across the barrier to explore this waterfall and what's at its base! (This last segment is up to you; the route shown on the book's map is just an approximation.)

When you can bear to tear yourself away from here, return the way you came.

Kahanu Gardens. . . . You may wish to add a stop at Kahanu Gardens to your visit on Ulaino Road. It's part of the National (formerly Pacific) Tropical Botanical Garden, chartered by Congress and headquartered on Kauai. The largest *heiau* on Maui, Piilanihale *heiau*, is on the grounds of Kahanu Gardens. Call ahead (808-248-8912) to find out if and when the gardens are open. There is an admission fee unless you're under 12 or a member of the National Tropical Botanical Garden.

Cascade on stream along Ulaino Road

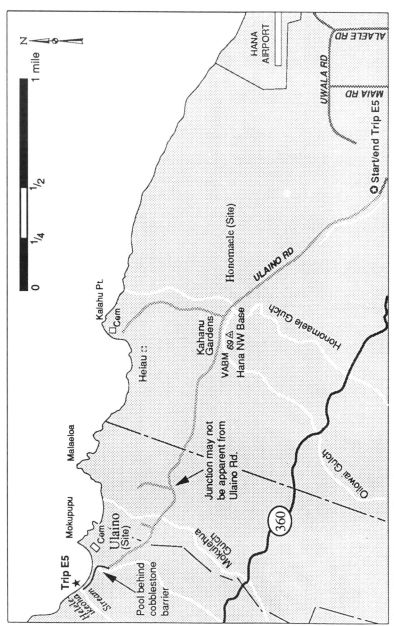

Trip E5. Ulaino Road.

Trip E6. Waianapanapa Cave
Side Trip from Hana

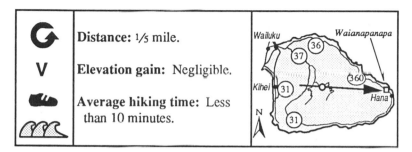

G	**Distance:** 1/5 mile.
V	**Elevation gain:** Negligible.
👟	**Average hiking time:** Less than 10 minutes.

Topos: *Hana 7½.*

Trail map (route approximated): At the end of this trip.

Highlights: This very short loop trip offers a chance to look into a cave whose floor is a pool of water and which figures in a famous and tragic legend (below).

Driving instructions: From Hana Beach County Park, drive back on Ua Kea Road north past the Hana Medical Center 2½ miles to the marked turnoff for Waianapanapa State Park, on your right. Follow this one-lane road ½ mile seaward to the park, then turn left and follow a very potholed road a little less than ¼ mile more past the tent-camping area to a parking lot, just under 3¼ miles total. All Waianapanapa State Park trips in this book (E6 through E10) start from this area.

Permit/permission required: None.

Description: A sign on the seaward edge of the parking lot points left (north) to the cave. You descend a paved trail and stairs under dense *hau* to the first of two fern-draped openings into the cave. The pool you see through this opening is sometimes reddish-colored from the millions of tiny shrimp that live in it. Continue ahead along the impatiens- and ginger-lined path, ascending some stairs, to a short spur path leading to a second cave opening. Walk the few steps down the spur to get a better look through this opening. The cave is said to have a second, dry chamber reachable only by swimming across the pool, as Popoalaea and her attendant did (below).

Now, back on the main path, ascend the next set of stairs past ferns, ginger, and *ti.* The path soon curves back to the parking lot, passing a sign with the cave's legend on it (see also below). You *could* leave Waianapanapa now, but I hope you'll stay to walk to the nearby overlook to enjoy the view of Waianapanapa's beautiful black-sand beach and sculptured sea cliffs—maybe even to take some more hikes!

Popoalaea. . . . As related by Martha Beckwith in her classic *Hawaiian Mythology*, the chief Kaakea received the Hana chiefess Popoalaea as his wife as a reward for his victory in a series of games that tested his strength. Kaakea was a very jealous man, and he was particularly jealous of Popoalaea's fondness for her younger brother. Hence, he was all too ready to believe false rumors about her infidelity, and he began sharpening his axe to kill her.

Popoalaea fled with her attendant, took refuge in the dry cavern at Waianapanapa above the pool of water, and secretively visited a nearby village at night for food. Unfortunately, the villagers reported the mysterious visitors to Kaakea. Their exact hiding place was not easy to find, but one day Kaakea saw on the water of the pool the shadow of the fly whisk the attendant was waving for her mistress. (Some sources say it was the reflection of Popoalaea's *kahili*, the feather-crowned standard of the *alii*, that Kaakea saw.) Kaakea seized and murdered both women.

It's said that when the water in the pool turns reddish, it's red with Popoalaea's blood. Each morning, it's also said, rainbow colors (*anapa*) play over the pool as a sign of Popoalaea's innocence. What a sad fate, but what a beautiful spot in which to be remembered.

Hala trees at **Waianapanapa**

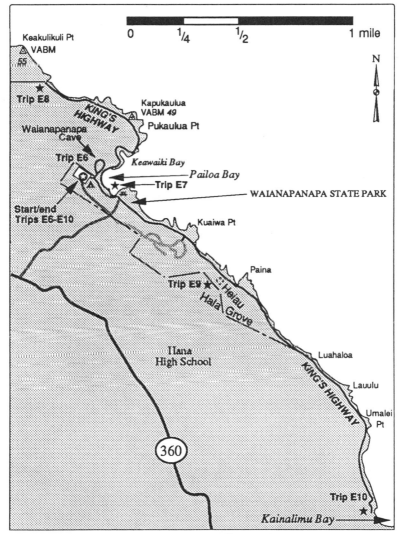

Trips E6-E10. Waianapanapa State Park.

Trip E7. Waianapanapa Black-Sand Beach
Side Trip from Hana

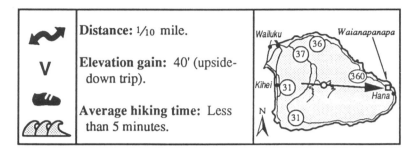

Distance: 1/10 mile.

Elevation gain: 40' (upside-down trip).

Average hiking time: Less than 5 minutes.

Topos: Optional: *Hana* 7½.

Trail map (route approximated): At the end of Trip E6.

Highlights: If you've been astonished at the beauty of Maui's many white-sand beaches, just wait till you see this gorgeous black-sand beach! A fair number of the people who gaze longingly at Waianapanapa's *black*-sand beach from the overlook near the parking lot seem unable to find their way down to it. Here's how to get to it.

Driving instructions: Follow the driving instructions of Trip E6.

Permit/permission required: None.

Description: From the seaward end of the parking lot, where the sign directs you left to the caves (Trip E6), turn right and head generally south on the path. Pause at the overlook of the black-sand beach to take in this glorious view. Among other lovely features, you'll count at least two natural arches in the cliffs cupping the beach. A few steps farther on, the path forks. The left fork here leads steeply down to the southeast end of the black-sand beach, which curves northwest away from the base of the path.

If you find the black-sand beach too crowded for your taste, there's a little black-*cobble* cove farther on. (The distance, elevation gain, and time given above don't include the jaunt to this cove.) Walk to the far end of the black-sand beach (away from the path you came down on). Here you'll find a little trail through the beach *naupaka*. Follow it upward through *hau, noni,* pink-flowered clover with sticky seeds, and sweet fern. After a brief level stretch, the trail descends to the black-cobble cove. Caution: swimming at Waianapanapa can be dangerous because of strong currents and high surf.

When you're ready, return the way you came.

Black-sand beaches. . . . are rare anywhere in the world. Most beaches are of light-colored sand. In the tropics, that usually means that the sand is pulverized coral—a gift of the sea. Black-sand beaches are a gift of the land. Some form when hot lava flows enter the ocean, causing a steam explosion that blows the molten material into millions of glassy fragments. You'll find a very few beaches like that on the Big Island of Hawaii; walking on their coarse sand is like walking on tiny beads of jet. These beaches are short-lived, as there's no reliable source of new material to replace what the ocean and the wind carry away. The fragments are the result of a single steam explosion. The chances of another flow occurring in the exactly the same place and in the same way, yielding similar fragments to replenish the beach, are very remote. The once-famous black-sand beach at Kalapana on the Big Island is all but gone now, its glassy sands swept away or blown inland. (It also suffered major damage when its section of coast abruptly sank about 3 feet in the powerful earthquake of November 1975.)

Other black-sand beaches are the products of erosion—particles of dark-colored material weathered from the rocks at the ocean's edge. That's the source of this black-sand beach here at Waianapanapa and at a few other sites in the Hawaiian Islands. The patient work of erosion has created not only those lovely arches and sea stacks from the surrounding black cliffs but also this beautiful little beach. As you can see, there's plenty of material left to erode, so *this* black-sand beach will be here for a little while.

Waianapanapa black-sand beach

Trip E8. King's Highway (North)
Side Trip from Hana

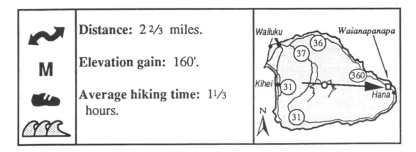

Distance: 2 2/3 miles.

M

Elevation gain: 160'.

Average hiking time: 1 1/3 hours.

Wailuku   Waianapanapa
36
37
360
Kihei 31
Hana
N
31

Topos: *Hana* 7½.

Trail map (initial route approximated): At the end of Trip E6.

Highlights: Scenery—the dramatic coastal scenery of the cliffs around Waianapanapa State Park and the sweeping views inland up the slopes of Haleakala. On your way, you visit the black-sand beach and black-cobble cove.

Driving instructions: Follow the driving instructions of Trip E6.

Permit/permission required: None.

Description: Follow Trip E7 down to the black-sand beach and over to the black-cobble cove. Cross the black-cobble cove and follow the trail as it climbs again, toward *hala* trees. With the help of a switchback, you're soon atop the cliffs in a region of twisted aa lava. The trail bears northeast through more *hala* and beach *naupaka* and follows the coast, passing high above bouldery Keawaiki Bay, where the waves surge in too forcefully for swimming. You pass through a forest of *hala* and find yourself in an open wilderness of aa lava, a landscape characteristic of the remaining coastal segments of the King's Highway (see below).

In ½ mile you reach a junction where you turn left (northwest); the right fork leads out to the remains of Kapukaulua VABM. If you pause for any length of time on this trail, you're apt to find your boots covered with a kind of ant that seems determined to conduct mass explorations of any stationary object. The rocks may be swarming with them, so keep your stops brief. You pass a small shrine, where you may wish to respectfully add your own stone. Continuing through the aa, the trail dips into a deep gully where, offshore, remnants of the sea cliff stand isolated, washed in turquoise water and white foam. You come out of one gully to descend into another. On the other side of the second gully, the trail may be quite faint. A little exploring will soon reveal the trail, and you follow it—very rough now—to a cove whose beach consists of large, rounded cobbles. Pick your way across the cove on the cobbles, then climb back up to the cliffs on a steep, very loose track.

You presently climb a little, pass a narrow natural arch, and reach an anticlimactic end at the chain-link fence around Hana Airport, 1⅓ miles from your start. It's time to turn around and retrace your steps.

The King's Highway. . . . is a remnant of old Hawaii, a trail around Maui established in prehistoric times for the king of Maui and his messengers and partly rebuilt in historic times. It's also called the *alaloa* or the *Hono a Piilani* Highway. Martha Foss Fleming, in *Old Trails of Maui*, estimated its original length at roughly 138 miles. Today, the hikable fragments are those that pass through aa fields here at Waianapanapa and east of La Pérouse Bay. Passage over the aa would have been very difficult if this trail had not been especially constructed. On easier terrain, the trail followed natural routes like beaches, and it has disappeared because there was never a *built-up* trail. Elsewhere, it's disappeared on account of erosion and neglect or been buried under newer construction.

Any lava field holds surprises no traveler needs. Fragile lava formations, such as thin ceilings over hidden lava tubes, can crumble underfoot, leaving you hanging in midair or, worse, falling. The King's Highway provides a safe passage through lava fields. The prehistoric Hawaiians invested a great deal of time and labor in building this roadway over the impossible jumble of the *aa* wilderness. As you'll find when you hike them, the waterless, shadeless *aa* fields can be brutally hot in the fiery sun. Imagine working to build the King's Highway in that heat, lifting and carrying the stones, placing them, and keeping the trailbed relatively level for all those miles.

These segments of the King's Highway can be demanding, for the *aa* rocks on the trailbed are loose and sharp. They roll around under your boots and make each step a little more work than you're used to. The trail makes no concession to the terrain. It simply marches as straight as it can steeply up, across, and steeply down the lava ridges and gullies. But look around you: what more could be done in this *aa* field without destroying it completely? Well done, I say!

Trip E9. Waianapanapa *Heiau*
Side Trip from Hana

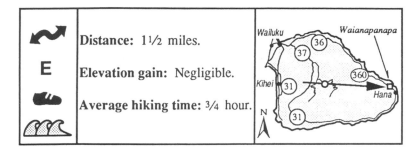

Distance: 1½ miles.

Elevation gain: Negligible.

Average hiking time: ¾ hour.

E

Wailuku   Waianapanapa
36
37
Kihei   31   360
Hana
31

N

Topos: *Hana* 7½.

Trail map: At the end of Trip E6.

Highlights: Magnificent scenery as in Trip E8; the coastal scenery is perhaps even better on this trip. Your visit includes the well-known *hala* groves of Waianapanapa, a fine, noisy blowhole, and a *heiau,* too.

Driving instructions: Follow the driving instructions of Trip E6.

Permit/permission required: None.

Description: Follow Trip E7 from the parking lot to the point where the trail to the black-sand beach forks left. Take the right fork here, quickly passing the tent campground and then a cemetery in the shade of tropical almond trees, to yet another fork. Go left at this fork, and you'll soon reach some picnic tables. This is a good place to pause to enjoy the view: the fresh tropical green of Haleakala's slopes, the black of Waianapanapa's basalt cliffs, and the foam-streaked blue-green of the sea. Notice the column-like formations in the cliffs; you'll see formations like these often along this coastal walk.

Now you descend a little as the trail winds past *aa* flows and through beach *naupaka* and morning glory. Dense groves of *hala* trees rise just inland of the path; often, the path is plentifully strewn with their long, sawtoothed, pointed leaves and their chunky orange fruit. Trails-of-use and even old roads strike off into the *hala* groves, but you stay on the coastal trail. Between ⅓ and ½ mile, listen for the roar of a big blowhole that's just seaward off the trail. When it actually "blows" depends on tide and surf (some wave combinations aren't strong enough to make it erupt), and it may take you by surprise. Look for low-lying strands of *akulikuli* in the rocks along your path here.

Near ⅔ mile, you cross a cement-reinforced bridge. Soon after that, you descend steeply but briefly beneath a tree heliotrope. At the bottom of this descent, the path continues between the tree trunk and a black rock face. At ¾ mile, you reach the *heiau*, a raised platform of black boulders. It's a picturesque spot, and you'll want to spend some time here. However, the lava field may be swarming with busy ants, so be prepared to defend your lunch.

When you're ready, retrace your steps from here. Or, if you feel the urge to go farther, continue toward Kainalimu Bay as described in the next trip.

Heiau, **graves, and shrines. . . .** These rugged and beautiful cliffs hold many sites of religious significance. Besides the *heiau* and the numerous small shrines, there are mounds of *aa* that may be ancient, raised graves. The leaf-wrapped rocks you're likely to see at this *heiau* are traditional offerings, and you'll probably see many such offerings as you hike the Hawaiian Islands. The traditional wrapping is a *ti* leaf, but here on Waianapanapa's cliffs, it's more often a *hala* leaf because there are no *ti* plants along the trail. There's a sense of the supernatural in the presence of so much natural beauty; perhaps the sounds of wind and waves carry echoes of ancient prayers chanted at these solemn places. It's easy to understand why even casual visitors today are moved to leave their own offerings here. Please treat all *heiau*, graves, shrines, and any offerings left at them with respect.

Beach naupaka

Trip E10. King's Highway South
to Kainalimu Bay Side Trip from Hana

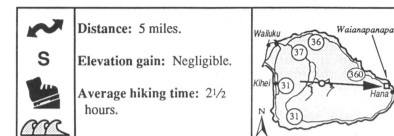

Topos: *Hana* 7½.

Trail map: At the end of Trip E6.

Highlights: More of the spectacular coastal scenery that makes Waianapanapa so unforgettable.

Driving instructions: Follow the driving instructions of Trip E6.

Permit/permission required: None.

Description: Follow Trip E9 to the *heiau*. A few yards beyond the *heiau*, a fence runs inland, perpendicular to the coast, and the King's Highway passes through it. Beyond this point, the King's Highway becomes rougher and fainter. At some points, you'll have to hunt around for it; please be careful in these sharp and sometimes unstable lava boulders. A telltale sign of the King's Highway that's particularly evident and useful here is a smooth boulder laid flat in the *aa* trailbed.

At a stretch of coast just over 1 mile from your start, look for a long sweep of coastal cliffs where the basalt columns are especially well-shaped, looking almost manmade—more about this below. Nearly 1⅓ miles from your start, you cross the end of a road that heads inland to your right; you continue along the King's Highway, which becomes even rougher now. The *aa*'s basic gray-black color is varied here and there by bands of red and brown and by whitish lichens, and the *aa* plain is broken by bizarre lava spires twisting skyward. Small ironwood trees grow here, their green foliage incongruously feathery and fresh against the dark, desolate lava.

Presently you cross a large field of smooth pahoehoe lava pocked by broken lava tubes and caves and invaded by beach *naupaka*. Here, you must follow ducks (small piles of rocks obviously set up by people) as the King's Highway is very indistinct. Don't fol-

low them blindly, though; test your next foothold to be sure it's sound
and will support you.

Nearing the 2½-mile point, you pass a sign that says
WAIANAPANAPA STATE PARK 3 MILES (it isn't that far). The track soon
dips into a buggy, tree-filled gully, where you may want a spider stick
to get past some hiker-size webs and their occupants. The track bears
left at the bottom of the gully and debouches at the cobblestone
beach of Kainalimu Bay. Rest here, enjoy this wild, lonely bay, and
then turn around and retrace your steps to your car.

Basalt columns.... When a lava flow forms a pond that cools
slowly, it may crack into column-like shapes like those you see here
along the Waianapanapa coast. Cooling lava shrinks, and cracks form
as sections of rock shrink apart. These cracks tend to go from the top
to the bottom of the cooling mass, producing the basic "column"
effect. The cracks intersect, and columns with from three to eight
sides form in the cooling mass. As every honeybee knows, a six-sided
structure is the most efficient, and six-sided columns tend to
predominate. A columnar formation is a spectacular sight when it's
exposed to view. Columnar formations are said to be rare on Hawaii,
so it's a special pleasure to see them here. (On the mainland, Devils
Postpile National Monument in California's Sierra Nevada includes
one of the better-known large columnar formations.)

Kings Highway at Kanaio

Trip E11. Hana Bay Side Trip from Hana

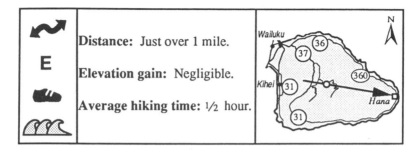

Distance: Just over 1 mile.

Elevation gain: Negligible.

Average hiking time: ½ hour.

Topos: *Hana* 7½.

Trail map (route approximated): At the end of this trip.

Highlights: A morning walk around Hana Bay offers fine views of Hana from the wharf and a chance to visit Kaahumanu's birthplace.

Driving instructions: This hike begins at Hana Beach County Park (see Trip E5).

Permit/permission required: None.

Description: Hana town *is* lovely, but it can get quite hot and humid. A long walk around Hana can be almost as debilitating as a walk through a steambath with hills. Add to this no sidewalks and streets with fast traffic that may come popping unexpectedly over the top of the hill you're walking on. I recommend that you keep your strolls in Hana town short, and restrict them to the early morning hours. With that caution, it's time to see Hana Bay.

Whatever direction you're facing when you get out of your car, it's hard to miss the prominent hill on the south side of Hana Bay, Kauiki (ka-oo-EE-kee) Head. Walk around the bay as it curves toward Kauiki Head. Follow the paved road as it bears left at the base of Kauiki Head at a little parking lot and out onto the wharf. Turn right where this first wharf meets a second wharf that runs almost at a right angle to it. Stroll out to the far end of the second wharf, a little over ¼ mile from your start, with a wonderful view of Hana town and its surroundings. A line of green-clad cinder cones marks one of Haleakala's rift zones. Nearer the town, a gray cross on sensuously shaped Puu o Kahaula honors the memory of Paul Fagan. When sugar production declined here and Hana's economy faltered in the 1940s, Paul Fagan helped revive Hana by introducing cattle ranching (Hana Ranch) and tourism (Hotel Hana-Maui). Grazing cattle dot the hillsides above the town now. And just in front of you, the blue waters of Hana Bay lap at the wharf.

Hana was one of the favorite places of the alii. Hana had everything, especially plenty to eat with little effort required to get food. The community maintained a lookout on Kauiki Head for schools of fish. Before Europeans came to Hawaii, Kauiki Head was covered with a native bunchgrass and could be climbed. Now, it's almost impossible to climb because of its dense cover of exotic plants. It's reported that the few who climb it get no reward for their effort: ironwoods block the view from its top.

Kauiki Head was used as a fortress; not surprisingly, it was the site of many battles. Hana is worth fighting over, and this isolated corner of East Maui has often been ruled by the Big Island of Hawaii. In 1754, the king of Hawaii conquered East Maui. Kahekili, then king of Maui, recaptured East Maui in 1775. The fortress at Kauiki Head did not fall in battle. Instead, Kahekili had to cut off the water supply to the fortress. When the fortress surrendered, Kahekili showed his contempt for the defenders by baking their bodies in earthen ovens.

As you'd expect, Kauiki Head also has its share of legends. One legend about the demigod Maui relates that long ago, the sky was so low that people couldn't stand straight. They even had to walk bent over. From the top of Kauiki Head, Maui pushed the sky up so that people could walk and stand upright.

Retrace your steps to the little parking lot at the base of Kauiki Head. A rough trail-of-use heads seaward (left) from here out onto Kauiki Head. Don't take it unless you have shoes with soles that will grip its unconsolidated surface. It's on loose red-cinder soil, and it quickly becomes steep and very narrow (it's very pretty, though). You contour around Kauiki's slopes through fern and *naupaka*, above a tiny red-cinder cove, and reach the plaque commemorating the birth of Queen Kaahumanu here in a cave in 1768. As outlined in "Geology and History, Natural and Human" in this book, Kaahumanu became Kamehameha's favorite wife, and after his death was a leader in overthrowing the *kapu* that had been the basis of Hawaiian social structure. Here's something to think about: how would Hawaii's history have been different if the *kapu* been in force when the first missionaries arrived?

A few more steps bring you to the little channel that separates Kauiki Head from Puukii Hill, on which a white lighthouse is perched, just over ½ mile from your car (including your walk out on the wharves). It's a wonderfully scenic spot. Remains of concrete piers suggest there was once a walkway across the narrow gap, but now you'd have to jump into the churning water and swim for it (not recommended). Instead, after enjoying the view, return to your car.

Around Hana. . . . A visit to Hasegawa's General Store was once a highlight of a stay in Hana town. The Hasegawa family had owned it since 1910. The little store was famous for having just about anything you could think of—and some you couldn't think of—in stock. It was "organized confusion," according to Harry Hasegawa, who had run the store for many years. "Of course we knew where everything was." But in August of 1990, Hasegawa's General Store mysteriously burnt down, reportedly during a dispute between developers and residents.[1] Some of Hana's aloha spirit probably went up in flames, too. Harry Hasegawa plans to reopen it in temporary quarters while a new store is being built. Perhaps the new store will be open when you visit Hana.

[1] Essoyan, Susan. "Fire at Hawaiian landmark reignites land fight." Los Angeles Times, September 3, 1990. The town's gas station burnt down at the same time in a separate incident. It's not known whether the fires are related to the dispute.

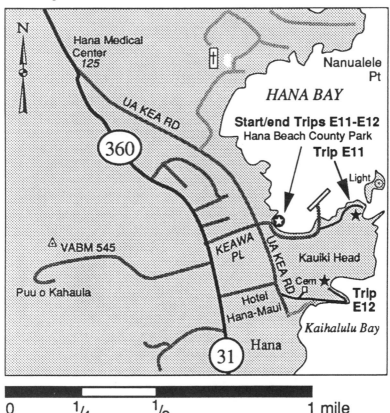

Trips E11-E12. Hana Bay and Red-Cinder Beach.

Trip E12. Red-Cinder Beach
Side Trip from Hana Town

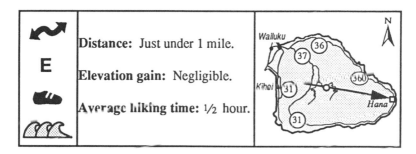

Distance: Just under 1 mile.

Elevation gain: Negligible.

Average hiking time: ½ hour.

Topos: *Optional:* Hana 7½.

Trail map (route approximated): At the end of Trip E11.

Highlights: Like black-sand beaches, red-cinder beaches are rare. This one, in a cove on Kauiki Head's south side, is a beauty. It's also called Red Sand Beach and Kaihalulu Beach. A natural break-water provides some extra safety for swimmers, and waves surging through it create what some call a natural jacuzzi. Because of Hana's heat, this is best as an early-morning walk. Note: While nudity is unlawful at any Hawaiian beach, there are a few beaches where it has been tolerated. This red-cinder beach is one of them. If nudity offends you, you may prefer another beach or hike.

Driving instructions: This hike begins at Hana Beach County Park (see Trip E5).

Permit/permission required: None.

Description: Return to the intersection of Ua Kea Road and Keawa Place. Turn south on Ua Kea Road (left if you're facing inland). There are no sidewalks, so please walk carefully and be alert for vehicular traffic. Proceed uphill behind Kauiki Head past the ballpark and the community center. Just on the other side of the community center, on the seaward side of the road, look for a grassy field with a chained-off vehicle access to an overgrown old road. (If you reach the Hotel Hana-Maui, you have passed the field; turn around.)

The overgrown old road helps you identify the field, but there's no point in following it. Just cut diagonally across the field toward a big ironwood tree on the south side of the field. Pick up a trail-of-use under this ironwood tree. This trail-of-use goes downhill toward the Hotel Hana-Maui, then turns to parallel the hotel's fence. At a junction, you take the right fork (the left leads to a tiny Japanese cemetery that's almost completely overgrown and very hard to spot).

The right fork continues along the hotel's fence and becomes quite steep. Watch your footing on this slippery little track; hold onto the fence if you must in order not to slip. It presently bears left and levels out, then fades out. When it does, bear left and climb a little (going right will *not* get you to the red-cinder beach). You pick up the track again and follow it under ironwoods. There's a fine view of Alau Island to the south from this stretch.

A little more than ⅓ mile from your start, you climb steeply, and the path is crunchy with fallen cinder particles. At another fork, the left fork continues to the beach (the right goes a few steps to another excellent viewpoint). You can see the beach from here, and it's a good place for a photo of it.

At last, you descend steeply to the beach, just under ½ mile from your start. It speaks for itself—eloquently. When you can bear to leave, return the way you came.

The red-cinder beach. . . . consists of—you guessed it—red cinders. They've eroded from Kauiki Head, which is a red-cinder cone, a product of Haleakala's last episode of volcanism. The cones formed by that episode stretch from Kauiki Head up Haleakala's slopes, forming the East Rift Zone, then across Haleakala Crater as the colorful cones for which the crater is so famous, and then down Haleakala's Southwest Rift Zone to La Pérouse Bay, south of Makena! Oxidized iron compounds give these cinders the warm brick-red color that's so striking against the cool blue-green of the sea.

Red-cinder beach, Hana

Trip E13. Oheo Gulch Pools
Side Trip from Hana

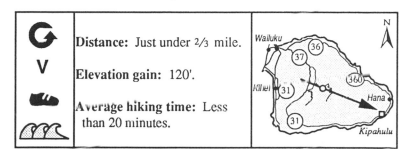

Distance: Just under 2/3 mile.	
Elevation gain: 120'.	
Average hiking time: Less than 20 minutes.	

Topos: Optional: Kipahulu 7½.

Trail map (route approximated): At the end of this trip.

Highlights: A splash in Oheo Stream's famous pools is what most people come here for. This is the area that was once erroneously referred to as the seven sacred pools. In fact, there are more than seven pools, and there's no evidence that they were ever considered sacred. But there's more to enjoy than the pools: Don't overlook the marvelous coastal views here. You can often see the Big Island of Hawaii across Alenuihaha Channel.

Driving instructions: From the intersection of Ua Kea Road and Keawa Place, drive uphill on Keawa Place and turn left onto the Hana Highway. From here, it's 10⅓ miles to the Kipahulu section of Haleakala National Park, which is where Oheo Stream is. At 7⅓ miles from Hana, you cross a bridge just inland of which beautiful Wailua Falls drops into a fine pool. You may be tempted to pull over onto the shoulder and walk back for a dip. On the road, you reach the park boundary, cross Oheo Stream, and follow signs a short distance to a dirt parking lot on the seaward side. In spite of its remoteness, enough people find their way to the Kipahulu section to fill this little parking lot to overflowing by midday. There are restrooms here but *no drinking water.* You must either purify any water you get from the stream or bring your own drinking water with you.

Permit/permission required: None.

Description: The marked trail to the lower pools begins at the northeast edge of the parking lot. You bear left round some picnic tables and then head downhill (east) toward the sea. You continue east (go right) at a trail junction, past Java plum and *kukui* trees, and cross a meadow dotted with clumps of *hala.* Soon you're on a bluff overlooking the ocean, next to the stone ruins of an old Hawaiian community. There are beautiful views up and down the coast and south-southeast to the Big Island.

Now the trail curves left (north-northeast) toward the stream, and it's just a minute or so before you hear the sounds of merriment from the pools. At the next trail junction, just over ⅓ mile from the parking lot, the right fork is a spur trail leading to views of the coast and, uphill, of Oheo Gulch. You take the left fork, and another trail junction pops up almost immediately. The right fork here will take you down steep stairs to the lowest pool. From there, you can work your way upstream to the other pools (not part of this hike). The pools are generally quite crowded.

The left fork (that is, continuing on the main trail) takes you uphill to an area where railings allow you to safely enjoy the view over the stream and snap some photos. *Hala, ti,* and sisal clothe the steep slope below your viewpoint. Continuing, you presently curve away from the stream under tropical almond trees, almost reaching the road. You could close this loop on the road, but it's nicer to turn left and take the trail, now on stairs for a short stretch, back to the parking lot. You pass a junction where you continue ahead (the left fork goes back to the stone ruins you visited earlier on this hike).

At ½ mile you reach another trail junction (it's the first one you passed at the beginning of this hike). Here, you turn right and soon reach the parking lot, a little less than ⅔ mile from your start.

While paddling in the pools. . . . keep an eye out for the water level. If it rises suddenly, that may indicate that a flash flood is imminent. Get out of the water immediately! You don't want to be swept downstream and drowned, much less be swept out to sea. It's said that the gray sharks around the mouth of Oheo Stream have acquired a taste for human flesh—a heck of a way to end your Maui vacation! But maybe sloshing around in the pools isn't all you're here for. *You'd* like to see some waterfalls! Read on—Trips E14 and E15 take you to splendid Makahiku Falls and then to enchanting Waimoku Falls.

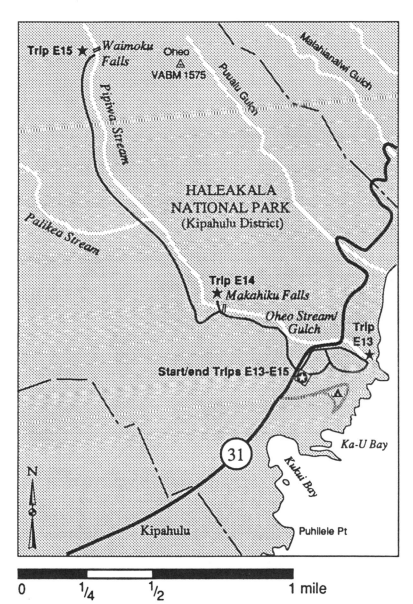

Trips E13-E15. Kipahulu District of Haleakala
National Park.

Trip E14. Makahiku Falls
Side Trip from Hana

Distance: Just over ¾ mile.

E

Elevation gain: 250'.

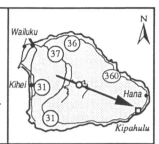

Average hiking time: 25 minutes.

Topos: *Kipahulu* 7½.

Trail map (route approximated): At the end of Trip E13.

Highlights: An easy hike through the lovely hills and pastures upslope of the highway brings you to an overlook of spectacular Makahiku Falls. You can swim off the dust of the hike in the fine pools behind the falls.

Driving instructions: Follow the driving instructions of Trip E13.

Permit/permission required: None.

Description: The trailhead for hikes uphill from the highway is across the highway from the parking-lot entrance, through a turnstile. You pick up the trail in the grass here and follow it northwest past mango, guava, and Christmas berry. The guava-hunting just off-trail is very good around here, but there are hazards (I emerged from the tangle of guava branches with a huge, bright-green praying mantis in my hair). You presently pass into some shade, then follow the trail as it bears generally west up a shadeless slope.

Near the ⅓-mile point, a spur trail leads right around some *hala* trees to a safety railing and an excellent view of Makahiku Falls. This is a good vantage point for a photo of the falls, too. Look for white-tailed tropicbirds soaring over the chasm. To the left of this viewpoint, a trail-of-use leads through a small, damp gully and down under Christmas berry and guava to the pools behind the falls. There's a good view seaward over the pools. Enjoy your swim here, and please observe the cautions given for the lower pools in Trip E13.

When you're ready, return the way you came.

Kipahulu Valley. . . . You've been hiking in lower Kipahulu Valley on this trail. If you look at a topographic map of Maui, the immense Keanae and Kaupo valleys will probably catch your eye.

You can see how they meet atop Haleakala to form Haleakala Crater. Now look to the east of Kaupo Valley, and you'll notice the deep "scoop" of Kipahulu Valley.

Kipahulu Valley is the result of distinct episodes of volcanism and stream-cutting. The first episode of volcanism built Haleakala. A second episode of volcanism covered the original volcano with new lavas. Rain soon sent streams radiating from the top of the shield volcano, cutting into it as they flowed. At Kipahulu, a stream carved a huge valley much deeper than the present one, cutting through both the newer and the older lavas. The next episode of volcanism sent new lava flowing down the huge valley, nearly filling it. A stream soon began cutting through the newest lava. Before this second stream could re-create the original valley by erosion, still more lava flowed from Haleakala, partly filling the newer valley. Now the present-day Palikea Stream, the western tributary of Oheo Stream, is scooping out the present Kipahulu Valley, while Pipiwai Stream, the eastern tributary of Oheo Stream, is scooping out a smaller side valley.

It seems likely that Palikea Stream will continue eroding Kipahulu Valley's headwall back toward Kaupo Valley and breach that wall, just as the streams forming Kaupo and Keanae valleys once breached their headwalls to create the crater—unless Haleakala erupts and fills Kipahulu again. In the meantime, a dense rainforest fills upper Kipahulu Valley, and many rare species of birds and plants flourish only there. Upper Kipahulu Valley is a scientific reserve closed to the public so that it can be protected, preserved, and studied.

The dense growth of the upper valley soaks up the abundant rain, releasing it in streams and springs and ensuring a good water supply for the settled areas below. The lands of Kipahulu are very productive. They once supported a large population and were, like Hana, fought over by the *alii*. Kipahulu was gradually abandoned as the center of commerce on Maui shifted to Lahaina in the early nineteenth century.

Trip E15. Waimoku Falls Side Trip from Hana

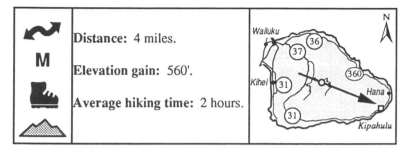

Distance: 4 miles.

Elevation gain: 560'.

Average hiking time: 2 hours.

Topos: *Kipahulu* 7½.

Trail map (route approximated): At the end of Trip E13.

Highlights: After your visit to Makahiku Falls, you continue uphill to Waimoku Falls. Along the way, you pass through stands of giant bamboo so dense that what little light filters down to you seems tinted green. Waimoku Falls is lovely, but the pool at its base is too shallow to swim in.

Driving instructions: Follow the driving instructions of Trip E13.

Permit/permission required: None.

Description: Follow Trip E14 to Makahiku Falls. If you want to swim, Makahiku Falls is a fine place to do so (Waimoku Falls isn't). Back on the main trail, you soon pass through a fence and bear north past some banyan trees. Your progress between here and the 1-mile point is apt to be slower than usual if you like guavas, for trees bearing abundant fruit line this stretch.

Nearing the 1-mile point, you cross an open area and descend slightly to pass through a fence and into a dense growth of guavas. A sign warns FLASH FLOOD AREA DO NOT CROSS DURING FLOODING and another warns you that it's a difficult trail ahead. Whatever the other hazards may be here, you're in very real danger of getting beaned by falling guavas as you stand reading these signs. Mosquitoes are sure to be a problem from here on, if they haven't been already, so apply that jungle juice now.

In a few more steps, you reach and cross Palikea Stream (a tributary of Oheo Stream) and scramble up very steeply under guavas and mangoes on the other side. Soon you're walking between walls of giant bamboo. Wooden walkways help you across boggy spots in and between these bamboo forests; watch out for missing planks. As you walk out of this first bamboo stand, clumps of fragrant yellow ginger line your path and the long ribbon of Waimoku Falls is straight ahead in the distance.

You descend the now-damp trail to another stand of bamboo, emerging from it into *kukui, ti, mamaki, and* thimbleberry. Now a third bamboo forest closes in on your trail, here very muddy and seeming to have just been hacked through the giant stalks. As you grope through the twilight of the dense stand, a breeze may rattle the stalks, playing random percussion music on them, and rustle the leaves, making a thin accompaniment with their whisperings.

On the other side of the bamboo, you cross a streamlet (watch the poor footing). In a few more yards, the trail becomes less distinct as you cross several channels of Pipiwai Stream flowing from Waimoku Falls, which you can see just ahead. Follow the trail or the channels a few more steps to the shallow pool at the waterfall's base, almost 2 miles from your start. Waimoku Falls is cradled in a deep little amphitheater with sheer walls to which cling mosses and ferns. Its base is surrounded by shattered rock; there's a real danger of rock-fall here. The principal cascade is on the left side, but smaller cascades slip down the walls on every side. Bands of solid lava rock alternate with looser bands of consolidated ash or clinker, layer upon layer up the amphitheater walls. Spray from the waterfall cools and dampens everything.

Rest awhile and enjoy this lovely sight. When you're ready, return the way you came.

Waterfalls at work. . . . In Hawaii, the terrain tends to consist of alternating layers of resistant lava and less resistant material, such as consolidated ash or clinker. The layers you see alternating in the amphitheater walls at Waimoku Falls are an example. A stream wears through the softer layer faster and cascades over the remaining harder layer. The force of the falling water wears away the rock at the base of the falls, forming a pool. Undercut by that process, rock above the pool succumbs to gravity and falls away, shattering at the base of the falls. This process wears the stream's channel farther and farther back into the slope. Over eons, the stream cuts its gorge back toward its headwaters. Because harder and softer layers alternate, many streams form a chain of waterfalls on their long descent to the sea. A waterfall like Waimoku may be—and in this case *is*—just one in the chain.

Trip E16. Kaupo Village to the Boundary of Haleakala National Park

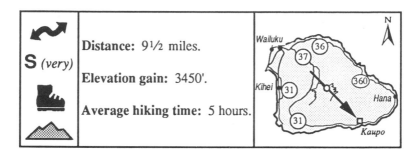

Distance: 9½ miles.

Elevation gain: 3450'.

Average hiking time: 5 hours.

Topos: *Kaupo* 7½.

Trail map (route approximated): At the end of this trip.

Highlights: The sweeping views down Haleakala's southern slopes from this steep, breezy, very strenuous trail defy words. The scene upslope to Kaupo Gap's mountain-guarded portals is just as stunning. A few miles east, scores of people crowd into the Kipahulu District parking lot to visit the pools and waterfalls of Oheo Gulch. But here at remote Kaupo, where there are no typical tourist attractions, you'll probably have the trail all to yourself.

Driving instructions: *You can't get to Kaupo from Kipahulu in the average rental car.* As mentioned earlier, much of the road between Kaupo and Kipahulu is unpaved and extremely rough. It's subject to washouts, landslides, and closures. If you must take it, check with the highway department first to see if it's open. If it's open, then tackle it only in a high-clearance 4WD vehicle with plenty of gas and well-stocked with food and water. There's no food, drinking water, or gas between Hana and distant Keokea (the Kaupo Store is rarely if ever open any more).

The better approach is from Ulupalakua, though it's a long and, beyond Keokea, a very slow drive. Allow at least 2 hours each way for this drive and have plenty of gas, food, and water with you. I'd prefer to have recommended that you make this a side trip from someplace closer than Wailuku. But there are very few accommodations and no legal campgrounds on the route between Kahului and the campground at Kipahulu. So it's drive, drive, drive; hike, hike, hike; drive, drive, drive!

From Wailuku, drive east on Highway 32 to Highway 36. Take Highway 36 southeast and then northeast to Highway 37. Turn onto Highway 37 southeast through Pukalani; stay on Highway 37 where

Highway 337 departs toward Haleakala's summit (both times). Follow it southeast, then south and southwest, through the rolling green slopes of "upcountry" Maui (Kula (Waiakoa), Keokea, and Ulupalakua Ranch). *Keokea is your last chance for gas!*

Beyond Ulupalakua Ranch, the road is renumbered as Highway 31 and bears east. It becomes much narrower; you may wish to pull over to let others pass from time to time. The speed limit along here is 15 mph. You descend gradually to the coast, and the pavement ends a little past Nuu. Start watching the highway mile markers, for your destination is the parking area in front of the Kaupo Store between mile markers 34 and 35, 49½ long miles from Wailuku. Park here without blocking anyone's gate or driveway.

Permit/permission required: None.

Description: Pause to take in the view from Kaupo Store's vicinity. The broad, flattened lava flow on whose seaward end you stand lies frozen in Kaupo Gap's throat, which is visible far upslope. To the east (right) of the flow lies deep Manawainui *Valley* (not the Manawainui *Gulch* you drove through on your way from Wailuku to Kaupo). Looking far up the valley, you may see water cascading in a long series of falls down its sides. That's as close as you'll get to a waterfall on this hike.

Walk about 300 yards farther east on the "highway" (right as you face Kaupo Store) and then turn left onto a corrugated, semi-paved road along which telephone lines run. Walk up this pleasant road between stone walls and fences, *koa haole,* Christmas berry, *kukui,* lantana, guava, and yellow-flowered be-still. The road bears left, then right, as it climbs gently and then moderately. Cow pies on the road speak of cattle ranching in the adjacent fields, and wind-sculpted trees attest to the constant strong breezes on this coast. You pass numerous gates but remain on the road.

A little over 1 mile from your start, the road forks at a stone wall; take the left fork, passing a few homes. If you're in luck, some of the native wiliwili trees along here may be sporting clusters of their large, softly folded, cream-to-golden-orange blossoms with long red stamens—a striking and increasingly rare sight. At 1⅓ miles, the road forks again; take the left fork (ahead) to the prominently marked beginning of the trail at a gate.

A sign a few yards past the gate advises you that you may go no farther on the road but must pick up the trail to your right (northwest). The ⅔ mile on this *foot* trail is slow—overgrown and sometimes hard to find. You pass juniper, mango, castor, and silk oak on the faint, grassy trail. The path isn't obvious, so numerous little

TRAIL signs point you to it. You cross an intermittent stream and ascend a slope, bashing your way through head-high grasses. The trail leads around a fence and passes an old trough as the grasses diminish. Now you work your way uphill into Christmas berry and *kukui* as the trail steepens. The understory is booby-trapped with lantana, and tracks diverge and converge frequently; you need the little TRAIL signs here. It *does* get better after this stretch!

You dip into a gully and then climb out steeply northward near a stone wall. A pass-through breaches a barbed-wire fence for you, and you shortly meet a 4WD road. Downhill to the right, a sign on a gate advises DO NOT ENTER DANGER WILD BULLS. You turn left toward a national park sign half-hidden in the vegetation. (The distance it gives to the park's boundary is wrong as of this writing—too short.) The road is a relief from the bushwhacking you've been doing, even though it marches steeply uphill. The road will occasionally relax its uphill march and noodle along the contours, but it's mostly uphill from here on.

At 3 miles, the road forks, and a crumpled sign currently suggests you should take the right fork downhill—*don't*. Take the left fork uphill past a water tank. You'll want to stop often to catch your breath on this steep climb and to enjoy the marvelous views in every direction.

As you approach the 4-mile point, the road forks twice. Take the left fork both times. At the 4-mile point, the maw of cloud-filled Kaupo Gap opens far uphill, and the peak named Haleakala rises on the Gap's west side. A patch of bare, red soil looms ahead of you. The road turns to parallel the patch of soil, carrying you into the shade of some *koa* trees, remnants of the forest that once clothed the upper slopes of Haleakala. You pass a water tank on your left.

At 4⅔ miles, you reach another road junction and again take the left fork (ahead). In a few more yards, amid plants uprooted by wild pigs, you reach the fence that now surrounds much of Haleakala National Park. A little flat spot with some avocado trees offers you a resting spot just outside the fence. Just inside the fence, a handsome grove of *koa* trees beckons you. If you go through the gate, *please be sure you close it, even if you have to stamp down the grass to do so!*

This trip ends here at the boundary of Haleakala National Park. Retrace your steps from here to your car. (Hikers who want to continue to Paliku Cabin should have a *Nahiku* 7½' topo and should reverse the steps of Trip H7.)

The road to Kaupo.... Cool, green "upcountry" is a treat for the eye and a welcome change from the heat of Lahaina and Kihei.

The eucalyptus-shaded fields and rolling green hills with their views down to the sea will seem very familiar if you've spent any time along the coast of central California.

A drastic change occurs after you pass Ulupalakua: the green pastures of "upcountry" abruptly disappear, and you find yourself driving through a landscape scorched, barren, and colorless in the fierce light. You drive past the barren Lualailua Hills and between the grazing lands of huge ranches. Cattle, stupefied by the heat and dazed by the glare, sag against splintering chutes and huddle in the pitiful shade of leafless *wiliwili* trees. Along the road, apple-of-Sodom's yellow fruit dangles fat and deadly from its withered parent. Now the road begins a definite descent to the coast, snaking in and out of the narrow throat of deep Manawainui Gulch.

These parched slopes once supported sizeable human populations. Not far from the Lualailua Hills and upslope of the highway lie the ruins of Kahikinui, where a thousand or more people once lived. *Maui: How It Came To Be* notes that there are more than 140 housesites in ruins between Ulupalakua and Kaupo. This area was heavily populated when Cook arrived in Hawaii in 1778. But soon after, the goats, cattle, and pigs descended from those brought by Europeans began stripping the land of its vegetation. It was naturally arid to start with; now, with insufficient vegetation to trap and retain what little moisture fell, it became a desert. The damage continues today; a way to successfully control the animals still hasn't been worked out (except for Haleakala's fences).

As you approach Kaupo, the green of trees softens the harsh landscape. Stretches of paved road alternate with unpaved road; then, a little beyond Nuu, the pavement ends for good. Sections of the road between here and Kaupo are covered with smooth beach pebbles that offer poor traction on the uphill side of some small rises. Don't fight it if you lose traction; roll back down and try another route up. The sound of pebbles ricocheting off the underside of a rental car may strike terror into your heart. At last you pass the Kaupo church and pull into Kaupo Store's tiny parking lot. Kaupo is beautifully green, swept clean by strong breezes, and tranquil in a way you're not likely to find elsewhere on Maui. Unlike Hana, Kaupo remains truly remote, difficult to reach, and little-visited.

Enjoy your hike, then leave quietly, thankful that there's still a place like Kaupo.

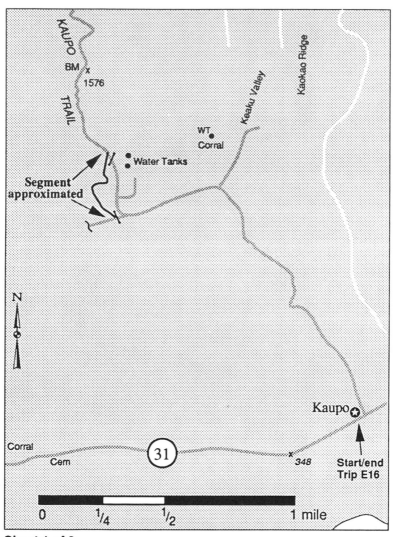

Sheet 1 of 2
Trip E16. Kaupo to Park Boundary (Sheet 1 of 2).

Continued on the map at the end of Trip H7

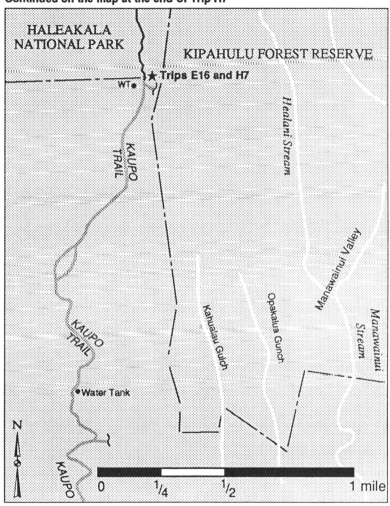

From Sheet 1 of 2

Sheet 2 of 2

Trip E16. Kaupo to Park Boundary (Sheet 2 of 2).

Trip E17. Fuchsia Wall Side Trip from Polipoli

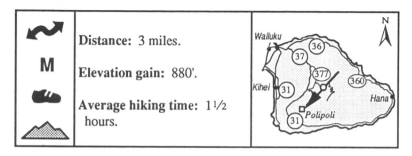

Distance: 3 miles.

Elevation gain: 880'.

Average hiking time: 1½ hours.

Topos: Optional: *Lualailua Hills, Makena* 7½.

Trail map: At the end of this trip.

Highlights: I have a surprise for you at the end of this trip, and I don't want to spoil it *here!* Okay, just a hint: flowers and birds.

Driving instructions: Polipoli State Park is so remote, partly because of the poor road to it, that it's almost mandatory that you stay overnight there. From Wailuku, drive east on Highway 32 to Highway 36. Take Highway 36 southeast and northeast to Highway 37. Take Highway 37 southeast through Pukalani and past the first (northern) junction with Highway 377 to the second (southern) junction with Highway 377, 19 miles. Turn onto Highway 377 (a very hard left) and drive ⅓ mile more to a junction with currently unmarked Waipoli Road on your right. It's the first road on your right that has a STOP sign. Turn right onto Waipoli Road.

Getting to Polipoli will take you another hour from here. Drive uphill on this road, ignoring side roads and driveways on your right. The road becomes quite steep, narrow (one lane; be alert for oncoming vehicles), and winding (one hairpin turn after another). Cattle graze alongside it; watch out for cattle straying onto the road. After 6 miles from the start of Waipoli Road, the pavement ends and the road, though less winding and steep now, is quite rough (protruding rocks and roots; sometimes deep dust, sometimes hard, slippery clay). Your rental-car company does not want you to drive this section, but, with care, it is just passable to ordinary passenger vehicles. The road forks 9½ miles from its start; bear right on the fork that dips downhill, negotiating a particularly rocky hairpin on the remaining ½ mile to Polipoli State Park's picnic and camping area. Park here, 29⅓ miles from Wailuku.

Permit/permission required: None.

Description: From the campground, backtrack a few steps through the parking lot and up the road to the side road that turns off north-northwest toward the cabin (left if your back is to the campground). You descend this barely discernable road, ducking under the vehicle barrier if it's closed. Soon you reach the cabin and curve around it on the road, then pass through an opening in a fence. At 1Z5 mile, you reach an obscure junction where you go right (northeast) onto a footpath, not left onto the road (which is currently marked THIS IS NOT A TRAIL). The footpath is the start of the Redwood Trail.

The damp path descends gently under conifers—look out for exposed roots on the path and for overhanging dead, cone-studded branches! This profusion of dead branches still on the tree, as well as the many fallen trees, gives the path that oppressive feeling of decay so characteristic of this forest. You twine down into the forest, eventually bearing west. Around ⅔ mile, look out for false trails leading northwest and south—you continue west for now. Not far beyond, a spur trail leads uphill on your left to one of Polipoli's must-miss shelter huts (see below). Just beyond ¾ mile, you reach a junction with the Tie Trail. Here, you and the Redwood Trail turn right and go north-northeast. Again, be alert for false trails as the Redwood Trail bears north.

Eventually, the Redwood Trail curves west. At 1⅓ miles, you reach an apparent junction with a false trail. The Redwood Trail with you on it continues ahead (southwest now; you'd have to make a hard right turn north-northeast onto the false trail). A few more steps bring you to the muddy, hydrangea- and fuchsia-filled yard of the decaying, garbage-filled "ranger's cabin" and then to a junction with the Boundary and Plum trails.

Turn right (northwest) onto the Boundary Trail and follow it past tall fuchsias—the "Fuchsia Wall"—for just under 1Z5 mile to some logs near the boundary fence, 1½ miles from your start. Have a seat here and look around you. The brilliant red sepals of the purple fuchsia blossoms have attracted one of Hawaii's native birds, the red *apapane*. At times, this wall of fuchsias seems almost alive with fluttering *apapane* sipping from the blossoms. In the evergreens behind you, look for a small greenish bird that gives a single *chirp!*, probably the Maui creeper (it's hard to spot until it moves).

Sooner or later, you have to tear yourself away from the Fuchsia Wall and retrace your steps.

Polipoli State Park. . . . is a wonderful resource for the people of Maui. They enjoy camping and hunting (pigs and goats) in its extremely dense, fog-bound forest of non-native trees: coast redwood, Oregon ash, cedar, eucalyptus, etc. For the people of Maui, that forest is a unique novelty.

That forest is one of the principal reasons why I think Polipoli is *not* a wonderful resource for *mainland* visitors. At the risk of offending the people of Maui, I see no reason at all for a visitor from the mainland to drive for hours on Maui to see a sickly forest consisting almost entirely of mainland species. Your time in Hawaii is limited, so spend it seeing things representative of Hawaii, not of the mainland!

There are three memorable hikes from Polipoli in this book: this one, E17, the Fuchsia Wall (which incorporates the forgettable Redwood Trail); E18, Kahua Road; and E19, Skyline Trail, which is also accessible from the summit of Haleakala. The other trails, including the hike known as the Polipoli Loop, are summarized in Appendix B of this book and are not worth your trouble, as explained below.

Polipoli's trails are in poor condition. There's a reason for this. The Division of State Parks and the Division of Forestry and Wildlife on Maui have limited funds, and trail maintenance isn't high on the list just now (preserving endangered ecosystems is, a choice that's hard to quarrel with). Polipoli's trails are being bulldozed out of existence by wild pigs, and there's not much anyone can do about it. Trails in the heart of the dense, non-native forest are very faint under their thick blankets of fallen needles and twigs and are further obscured by a maze of crisscrossing trails-of-use. In the fog or in the dark—forget it! At their best, they would still be uninteresting: you can't see much besides a dense network of dead twigs ahead of you. Potential views at the occasional openings are often concealed by the daily fogs. Most of Polipoli's trails don't appear as trips in this book for these reasons.

The plum trees some sources mention as a Polipoli attraction are mostly gone—shaded to death in the incredible overgrowth that, together with Polipoli's normal daytime fog, makes it twilight at high noon under the redwoods, ash, cedar, eucalyptus, etc. The overgrowth of the forest is largely due to the spacing of the original plantings in the 1930s by the Civilian Conservation Corps. It's hoped that as stronger trees crowd out and kill weaker trees, a healthier, more open forest will eventually take the place of the present one.

If you do hike in the heart of Polipoli, make sure you get back to your camp or your car before sunset. The brief Hawaiian twilight is as dark as night there, a bright moon can't penetrate the forest except at rare clearings, and a flashlight is no substitute for daylight in that dense growth and on those faint trails. (You should still carry one, anyway.)

Staying at Polipoli. Polipoli State Park is very remote, very wet, and very cold compared to the rest of Maui. (It lies in a local low spot within Haleakala's inversion-layer cloud bank.) Your choices when you stay overnight there are its tiny tent-campground or its one cabin (reserved through the Division of State Parks; book well in advance). Drinking water is available only at the tent-campground and the cabin. The shelters along the trails do not merit your consideration. They are either windowless wooden huts with no light, no water, four dirty wooden bunks, and dirt—I mean loose dirt!—floors, or they are claustrophobic caves. Your tent is a palace compared to those shelters.

Your tent must be waterproof, as it rains frequently at Polipoli and is always damp there. You'll need a warm sleeping bag, rain gear, and plenty of warm clothing. The nearest lodgings are in Kula on Highway 377, but even from there, it's an hour-long grind each way to/from Polipoli.

Hang glider taking off from Polipoli Road

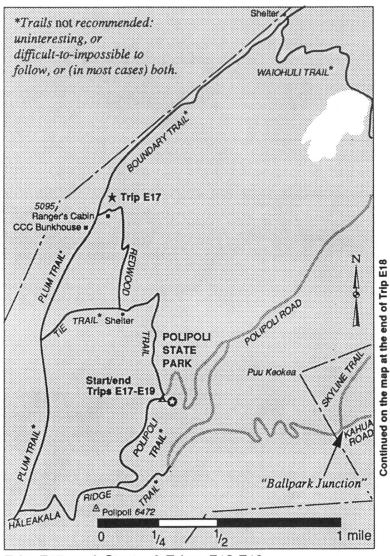

*Trails not recommended:
uninteresting, or
difficult-to-impossible to
follow, or (in most cases) both.

Shelter

WAIOHULI TRAIL*

BOUNDARY TRAIL*

★ Trip E17

5095;
Ranger's Cabin
CCC Bunkhouse ■

PLUM TRAIL*

REDWOOD TRAIL

TIE TRAIL* Shelter

POLIPOLI ROAD

POLIPOLI
STATE
PARK

Puu Keokea

SKYLINE TRAIL*

Start/end
Trips E17-E19

N

PLUM TRAIL*

POLIPOLI TRAIL

KAHUA ROAD

RIDGE TRAIL*

"Ballpark Junction"

HALEAKALA

△ Polipoli 6472

0   1/4   1/2   1 mile

Continued on the map at the end of Trip E18

Trip E17 and Start of Trips E18-E19.
Polipoli State Park.

Trip E18. Kahua Road Side Trip from Polipoli

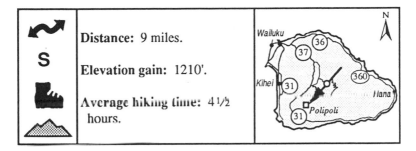

Distance: 9 miles.

Elevation gain: 1210'.

Average hiking time: 4 1/2 hours.

    Topos: *Lualailua Hills 7½.*
    Trail map: Starts on the map at the end of Trip E17; ends on the map at the end of this trip.
    Highlights: Easy going through native scrublands on an old 4WD road with views upslope to Haleakala's summit region and downslope to the ocean (weather permitting). This is by far the most enjoyable of the trails that are accessible *only* from Polipoli State Park (more below). Kahua Road is a fine choice for mountain bicycles, too.
    Driving instructions: Not applicable if you're already camped at Polipoli State Park. Otherwise, follow the driving instructions of Trip E17.
    Permit/permission required: None.
    Description: You could start this trip on Polipoli's poor trail system, but I found it much more enjoyable to start on the road. I think you will, too. Get an early start so you can enjoy the views before the fog moves in (it will probably be in a layer just below the road).
    Walk back ½ mile on the road you drove in on, to the fork where you turned right to get down to Polipoli. Take the other fork here (a sharp right) and continue uphill. The elbow of a hairpin turn at 1 mile from the start offers wonderful views over the ocean to Molokini and Kahoolawe, even a glimpse of the Big Island of Hawaii, if cloud-cover permits. One of Polipoli's trails, the Haleakala Ridge Trail, meets the road at this elbow.
    Volcanic material lies exposed in the road cut, in some places as stacks of wafer-thin orange, black, and tan layers. Near 2 miles, you reach a fork in the road at what's called Ballpark Junction. (The Civilian Conservation Corps men who planted the present forest in the 1930s used to play softball on this flat, open spot.) Kahua Road is

the righthand fork, which you take (the lefthand fork is Skyline Trail to Science City atop Haleakala—see Trip E19).

On Kahua Road now, you ignore any tracks leading away from the road, which rises very gently as it heads generally east. The non-native forest soon disappears, and native plants begin to dominate, particularly red- and white-berried *pukiawe*, red-fruited *aalii*, and red-berried *ohelo*. Be sure to look up at that wonderful line of cinder cones along Haleakala's southwest rift zone from time to time—quite a sight! The road passes through flows of rough *aa* lava as clouds move constantly across the slopes, now hiding, now revealing, but always leaving a strip of blue sky *somewhere*. Cool breezes make this exposed road quite pleasant. Here and there, masses of concrete lie broken where there's been an unsuccessful attempt to smooth the road's rough surface. You'll also notice the occasional rain-collecting station's roofs and tanks.

A little past 3 miles, the road begins an almost imperceptible descent, cutting through low ridges of brown *aa* that extend like misshapen fingers toward the distant sea. Scrub and bracken fern happily colonize them. It's not long before you can see a bit of the white towers and domes of Science City, the research complex atop Haleakala, uphill and to the left (northeast), if weather permits. The slopes below Science City are streaked with colors: brick reds, browns, deep maroons, tans, touches of pink and orange, and the green of vegetation.

You've been seeing lots of *aa* lava, but just past 4 miles, there's a smooth pahoehoe lava flow. A little farther on you'll find Kahua shelter (on the left side of the road; water available outside) and a pit toilet and Kahua cone (on the right). The deteriorating road passes behind Kahua cone and ends at a trashed-out grassy area 4½ miles from Polipoli. A footpath, the Kahikinui Trail, takes off east-south-east from here through the lava fields; its start is marked only by a couple of metal poles (more about the Kahikinui Trail below).

From here you retrace your path back to Polipoli.

Kahikinui Trail. . . . is an interesting and very rugged trail-of-use. It's so remote that if you wish to explore it, you should backpack out to the end of Kahua Road and camp near Kahua shelter, sharing its pit toilet and drinking water supply with anyone staying in the shelter. That would give you time to really enjoy the Kahikinui Trail. Check with the Division of Forestry and Wildlife for permission to camp out there (or, at least, assurance that it's okay to do so, as it was when I checked in October of 1990).

I explored the Kahikinui Trail for about 1½ miles, probably as far as Manawainui Gulch, but not to its end (at least another ½ mile), for lack of time. There were not enough landmarks I could recognize in order to better determine my location at my turnaround point.

The trail-of-use leads across the pleated southern slopes of Haleakala some 5000 to 6000 feet above the scorched countryside through which Highway 31 passes as it goes from Ulupalakua to Kaupo. This is a hunting area, and trash from hunting parties litters the track. The trail occasionally becomes quite hard to follow, so you need to orient yourself with the large cairns (piles of rocks) built on the larger ridges. At times you need to employ your boulder-scrambling skills. You climb over one lava ridge and descend into the gully beyond it, climb out of the gully onto the next lava ridge and descend into the next gully. . . . That might seem monotonous, but something interesting unfolds: the farther you go, the larger and deeper the gullies are, and they begin to hold pools and even streams of water. The floors of the deeper gullies are very smooth in contrast to the rough *aa* of the ridges, and there are interesting formations in some of them. As the gullies become more moist, they provide a niche where soil has accumulated and red-flowered *ohia* trees have taken root. Successive niches seem to support a wider variety of plants. I don't know what you'll find at its end or how you'll know you've reached the end. A current rumor says that the Kahikinui Trail may be extended even farther, perhaps by volunteers.

See the supplemental information at the end of Trip E16 for a brief look at the ecology and history of these slopes.

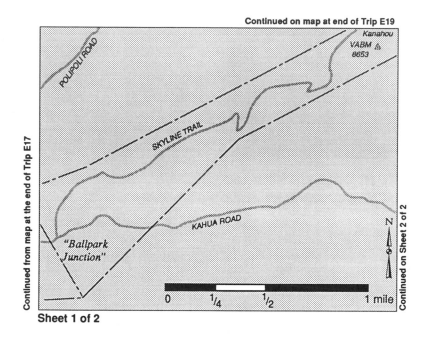

Continued on map at end of Trip E19

Sheet 1 of 2

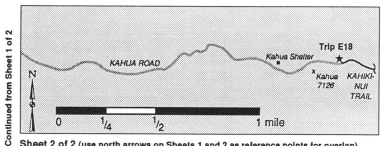

Sheet 2 of 2 (use north arrows on Sheets 1 and 2 as reference points for overlap)

Trips E18-E19 (Continued). Kahua Road and Skyline Trail.

Trip E19. Skyline Trail Side Trip from Polipoli

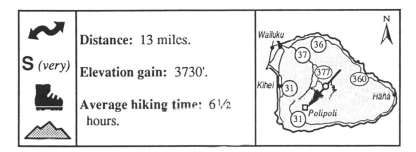

S *(very)*

Distance: 13 miles.

Elevation gain: 3730'.

Average hiking time: 6½ hours.

Topos: *Lualailua Hills, Kilohana* 7½.

Trail map: Starts on the map at the end of Trip E17; continues on the map at the end of Trip E18; ends on the map at the end of this trip.

Highlights: This thrilling walk up Haleakala's southwest rift zone to Science City, the research complex atop Haleakala, offers sweeping views along Haleakala's slopes and down over the isthmus to West Maui (weather permitting). The contrast between the overgrown Polipoli region at the start and the lava moonscape at the top is startling. Nearing the top, the road wanders among cinder cones and vents—at least one big vent opens almost at your feet. Most of the Skyline Trail is now closed to motorized traffic, so it makes an outstanding hiking and mountain-bicycling trail. *This* would be the way to bike down Haleakala—no dodging the stream of passenger vehicles! Of course, you can also hike or bike the Skyline Trail down from Science City and then back up (see the end of Trip H17).

Driving instructions: Not applicable if you're already camped at Polipoli State Park. Otherwise, follow the driving instructions of Trip E17.

Permit/permission required: None.

Description: Follow Trip E18 to Ballpark Junction. Take the left fork and climb moderately past orange-berried *pilo*, yellow-flowered *mamane, pukiawe, ohelo,* bracken fern, and dubautia. Note the dubautia, with its composite brush of yellow florets. It's a relative of the silversword (hard to believe, but it's true; more on this following Trip H10).

The Skyline Trail stays on the northwest side of the rift zone most of the time. On the ridge to your right, the line of red-brown cinder cones marches along the rift itself. Early in the morning, you have breathtaking views downslope across "upcountry," where plantings of conifers look like so many toy Christmas trees. You'll notice the occasional rain-catching station, too (roof, tanks). Many roadside cuts display colorful layers of volcanic soil. It's possible you'll see wild pigs here, along with ring-necked pheasants. Non-native evening primrose (large, loose, yellow flowers) and thistle put in an appearance, too.

You can't help but notice as you rise higher and higher that the vegetation becomes smaller and sparser. At 3¾ miles you pass around a gate that bars further travel to motorized vehicles, and soon the larger shrubs disappear. Nearing 5 miles, only *pukiawe* remains, in low, compact mounds. Up here, the ground is covered with red, gray, orange, and pink volcanic cinders. On them lie raw chunks of red and black-red rock—"lava bombs," masses of lava ejected from the adacent vents. Here and there between the heaps of lava grow strange little alpine meadows of tough straw-colored grasses, low dubautias, and diminutive bracken ferns. The jagged mouths of vents gape north and east of you. As tempting as it may be, exploring lava fields off-road or off-trail can be hazardous without a knowledgeable guide. You could unknowingly step right through the fragile roof of an unseen lava tube. Mountain-bicyclists should carefully control their speed on this section, where the roadbed consists of very loose material.

You leave Kahikinui State Forest Reserve at 6 miles and pass around the upper road-closure gate just before 6½ miles. Another few steps bring you to the Skyline Trail marker for the upper (Science City) end. Depending on your fancy and the weather, you may want to find a spot in the cinders near here to rest, enjoy the available views, and have lunch. Or you may want to continue carefully up the road to the observation shelter at Red Hill, visible straight ahead now (additional mileage and elevation gain not included in the figures for this trip).

When you're ready, retrace your steps back to Polipoli.

Why are Puu Kukui and Haleakala so different? . . . As you walked up from Polipoli, you probably had good views of West Maui until the daily cloud layer formed. Puu Kukui, the volcano that created West Maui, is one of the wettest spots on earth, as its deeply eroded contours brilliant with dense rainforest growth attest. For rainfall, Puu Kukui (5788 feet) rivals Kauai's Mt. Waialeale (5148 feet), which is considered by some to be the rainiest spot on earth. Puu Kukui and Mt. Waialeale have features in common that make them so rainy. Continuing on the Skyline Trail, you then walked up through scrublands and into the alpine desert near the top of

Haleakala, where only a few low plants are tough enough to survive. How different Puu Kukui and Haleakala are! But why? In *Hawaii: A Natural History*, Sherwin Carlquist gives an explanation that I've tried to summarize here.

First, an oversimplified look at the air over Hawaii: The Hawaiian Islands tend to have daytime inversion layers 50% to 70% of the time. In these inversion layers, the air gets warmer as it rises (the land heats it). The top of the inversion layer is at 5000 to 7000 feet. Above, there's cooler air. Second, the incoming winds, both trade and kona, pick up a great deal of moisture on their long sweep across the open ocean to Hawaii. The winds rise, warming instead of cooling as they rise, until they encounter the cooler air at the top of the inversion layer. There their moisture condenses as rain.

If the mountain is rounded and its summit is at about the height of the inversion layer, the moisture-laden air rises gradually. The moisture condenses as it rises up and over the summit. There's time for rain to fall on the windward and leeward sides as well as on the summit.

That doesn't happen with Puu Kukui and Waialeale, even though both summits are at about the height of the inversion layer. Both mountains have rainfall concentrated near the summit and have dry leeward sides because both mountains are not rounded. They're gashed on all sides by deep, narrow valleys that have very steep headwalls. The moisture-laden winds rush into those valleys and fly up the steep headwalls so rapidly that the air mass is almost at the summit when the moisture condenses very abruptly. Most of the rain falls on the summit ridge and just beyond the summit, effectively concentrating the rainfall in a relatively small region. Immense swamps lie just beyond these summits.

If the mountain is significantly higher than the inversion layer, the rain falls largely on the windward side, leaving both the summit and the leeward side dry. This is the case with 10,023-foot Haleakala. You can almost see the top of the inversion layer around Haleakala. A cloud layer typically forms in the morning and surrounds the mountain at about 5000 to 7000 feet on most sides. Polipoli State Park at 6200 feet on the western slopes lies within this cloud belt, and it is usually very foggy, often rainy, by mid-morning. Above the inversion layer lie the drier scrublands and the alpine deserts you walk through on the Skyline Trail.

The Skyline Trail, with its views of Puu Kukui, offers a fine lesson about Maui's "weather makers" and their effects—a lesson you can take with you to help you better understand the other Hawaiian islands, too.

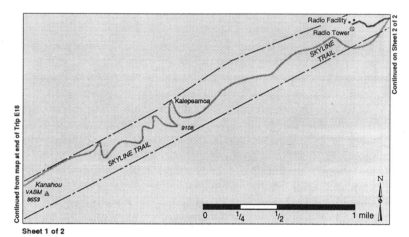

Sheet 1 of 2

Trip E18 (End). Kahua Road.

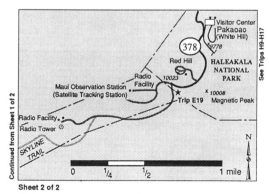

Sheet 2 of 2

Trip E19 (End). Skyline Trail.

Trip E20. King's Highway to Kanaio

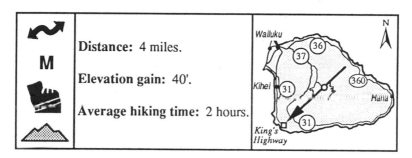

Distance: 4 miles.

Elevation gain: 40'.

Average hiking time: 2 hours.

Topos: *Makena 7½.*

Trail map: At the end of this trip.

Highlights: An unforgettable panorama: the dazzling turquoise-blue of the water along this coast as seen across the tormented *aa* landscape left by Haleakala's most-recent eruptions.

Driving instructions: From Wailuku, drive south on Highway 30 to its junction with Highway 31 to Kihei, Wailea, and Makena. Turn left onto Highway 31 and follow it past Maalaea Beach and Kealia Pond. As you pass the northernmost condominiums in Kihei, the highway swings slightly inland at a junction with South Kihei Road, 8½ miles from Wailuku. Turn right onto South Kihei Road and follow it south through Kihei. As you approach Wailea, you turn inland (left) a short way on Okolani Drive, then right on Wailea Alanui. You pass several large resorts and golf courses as the road becomes Makena Alanui. As you near the end of the Makena Golf Course, the road becomes very narrow, and thickets of *kiawe* stretch away on either side of the road. You pass a couple of dirt roads leading seaward to Puu Olai (Trip E21). The road is alternately paved and unpaved now—more often paved—and bobs up and down. You may not be able to see traffic on the other side of these "mounds," so exercise caution. The road presently dips down to skirt Ahihi Bay and then crosses the base of Cape Kinau to a small parking area just below Puu o Kanaloa at the northwest end of La Pérouse Bay. From here the "road" is impassable to all but the stoutest 4WD vehicles and to the Ankle Express, so park here to begin your hike, 23¼ miles from Wailuku.

Permit/permission required: None.

Description: The heat from the sun, reradiated by the dark lava rocks along this route, can be intense, and there is no fresh water. From the parking area, pick up the extremely rough 4WD

road that bears southeast over *aa* and under *kiawe* to skirt La
Pérouse Bay—don't take the spur road that goes south to the sea.
There are wonderful views over the blue-green bay toward
Kahoolawe and up the slopes of Haleakala, down which streams of
rough, dark lava have poured. The road soon becomes sandy and
begins winding in and out of tiny, rocky coves under a natural arch-
way of *kiawe*. Inland, growing *kiawe* pushes apart the lichen-speckled
boulders of old stone walls.

The road becomes alternately rocky and sandy, and *hau* and
noni appear as you pass the ½-mile point and reach a little beach. At
a junction (not on the map) on the far side of the little beach, take the
right (south-southeast) fork through an open area of reddish *aa* and
past a square stone enclosure seaward of your route. Where the road
bears seaward to the light on Cape Hanamanioa, a little more than ⅔
mile from your start, you notice a stone wall on your left (inland).
Look for a pedestrian opening with a vehicle barrier in the wall and
turn left (inland) through the pedestrian opening. Walk about 100
feet to the Hoapili Trail, built in its present form by Governor
Hoapili in 1824–1840. (Remember that these lava flows date from
about 1790, so they may have destroyed an earlier King's Highway
here. See Trip E8 for some background on the King's Highway.) Na
Ala Hele, the Hawaiian trail-support organization, has rebuilt
Governor Hoapili's "King's Highway" here, and you turn right onto
it.

The going is pretty rough now, as the trail consists of *aa* chunks
laid to form trailbed but not cemented together, so that they wobble a
little under your boots. The *aa* wilderness stretches away on all sides,
often blocking ocean views. Its origin in the lava flows on the slopes
above could hardly be more obvious. *Is this what an ant feels like in a
gravel bed?* you may wonder. Still, the tortured rocks are not without
their beauty. They are, after all, the raw material from which time
and erosion will fashion new, fertile plains. Some of the rocks ring
almost bell-like beneath your feet. Stop to examine them. The broken
fragments sometimes reveal delicate, marbled colors and bubble
chambers. Grays and browns predominate, but surprising tints
appear when you look closely: soft oranges, deep purplish reds, brick
reds, ochres, pinks, and the white of lichens called "Hawaiian snow."
Rarely, you may see a smooth lava "bomb."

Two miles from your start, you descend very abruptly to a marvelously picturesque, *kiawe*-shaded cove along a coast locally known
as Kanaio. There is a trashy campsite here, and a 4WD road comes
down to it on the far side. Still, it's a fine place to rest and have lunch.

The King's Highway continues a few coves farther on, but this trip ends here. Retrace your steps when you're ready.

Beyond Kanaio. . . . You may want to explore Kanaio a little more before you leave. If you continue along the shore, you'll hear the *WHOOOOOSH!* of a small blowhole if the tide is high enough. (I'll let you have the fun of hunting for it.) Your trail is a 4WD road now; as you approach a ruin on a small point, it turns inland. At a junction with another jeep trail, one that goes inland, you bear right (east), staying along the coast. It becomes rockier and, at 3 miles, dips abruptly down through a stone wall toward the sea.

I cannot recommend the next stretch to Kanaloa. The King's Highway has not been rebuilt here and is extremely rough and hot. You are permitted to backpack this route and to camp along this coast from Kanaio east to Kanaloa, but I can't recommend that, either. There's no fresh water, and the few potential campsites are full of junk.

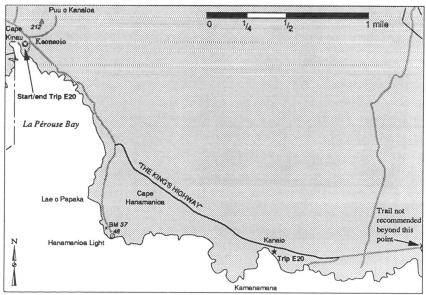

Trip E20. King's Highway to Kanaio.

Trip E21. Puu Olai

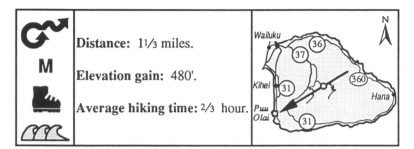

Distance: 1⅓ miles.

Elevation gain: 480'.

Average hiking time: ⅔ hour.

Topos: Optional: *Makena* 7½.

Trail map (route approximated): At the end of this trip.

Highlights: Superb views from one of the two summits of this little tree-topped cone, plus an opportunity to visit two beautiful beaches.

Driving instructions: Start as described in the driving instructions of Trip E20, but don't go all the way to La Pérouse Bay. As you drive south from Kihei, you can't miss the hill—Puu Olai—that's almost out in the ocean. Start looking for the unmarked turnoff to Puu Olai after a paved road comes in from the north to join Makena Alanui at a very sharp angle on your right, just as the main road turns away from Makena Golf Course. Pass the first *dirt* road on your right (seaward) (it goes to the north side of Puu Olai and is very, very rough). The next dirt road on your right, which is obviously near the south side of Puu Olai, is the one you want. It's in pretty good shape as of this writing. Follow it for almost ½ mile to the parking area near the elevated restroom (yes, I thought it was a lifeguard tower, too) at the north end of Ahihi Bay, 20½ miles from Wailuku. The beach in front of this parking area is locally known as Big Beach; some maps show it as Oneloa Beach. Park here or as close as possible. Vandalism is, unfortunately, very common here, and cars are probably more vulnerable the farther they are from the beach, where people are more likely to be. Your chances of parking right at the beach are better in the early morning; this beach is very crowded later in the day.

Permit/permission required: None.

Description: Walk past the elevated restroom toward the handsome red cliffs framing the north end of the beach. The little point extending from the base of Puu Olai is right ahead of you; walk to its face. Here you'll find a steep trail-of-use hidden in the cliff. You

scramble steeply up the low cliff with the help of some natural handholds. When you're atop the cliff, take the time to look back and
enjoy the view of Big Beach from here. Side trails lead out onto the
point to tidepools, and a wide trail leads northwest (ahead) to Little
Beach. You, however, want the very steep trail-of-use on your right
that climbs northeast along Puu Olai's southern slopes. Take this
trail upward—*upward!*—on loose, cindery soil, through *koa haole*
and *kiawe*. Past the ⅓-mile point, the grade eases a little, then
steepens again as you pass through weeds, and finally eases for good
at an open spot a little over ½ mile from your start.

Here, atop Puu Olai's southeast summit, you have fabulous
views southwest to Molokini and Kahoolawe, northwest to West
Maui, southeast to Haleakala, and south to the southwest rift zone
and Cape Kinau. Now you begin the loop part of this trip by following the trail-of-use north past a slight depression and through
scrub, to a fork. Take the left fork, which passes a cement marker
(possibly the remains of the benchmark shown on the topo), descends to a saddle, and then climbs to Puu Olai's northwest summit.
Though it's slightly higher, this summit's views are obscured by
kiawe and the southeast summit. Follow the track across this summit as it descends west and then south around Puu Olai's *kiawe*-filled
vent. At the low point, you meet a track coming uphill from the west,
but you continue south around the crater, ascending to the open spot
on the southeast summit.

Retrace your steps down Puu Olai—slippery on this steep grade
and loose soil. From here, you can retrace your steps to lovely Big
Beach (left as you face the ocean). If you turn to your right, the trail
leads to Little Beach in a few dozen yards.

When you're ready, return the way you came, just over 1⅓
miles total (not including going to Little Beach).

Little Beach. . . . *Hawaii's Secret Beaches* says that Little
Beach is "Hawaii's most well known nudist beach because of the
numerous arrests here of nudists." It is beautiful, and, though nudity
is officially illegal here because it's in a state park, you'll find people
sunning and swimming with and without swimsuits. If nudity
offends you, it's best not to go to Little Beach. Nudity isn't legal anywhere in Hawaii, but there are a few very remote places where it's
tolerated.

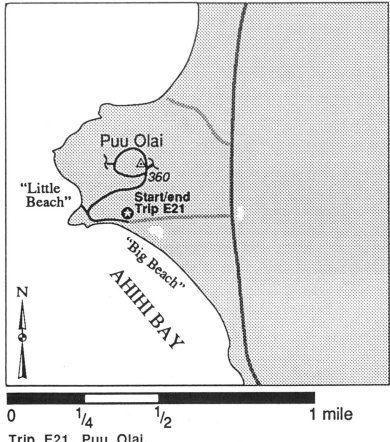

Trip E21. Puu Olai.

Trip E22. Polo Beach

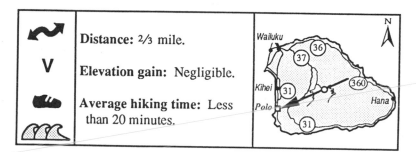

Distance: 2/3 mile.

Elevation gain: Negligible.

Average hiking time: Less than 20 minutes.

Topos: Optional: *Makena* 7½.

Trail map (route approximated): At the end of this trip. There is no trail as such; you walk along the beach as you please.

Highlights: This trip: 1. Gives you an excuse to visit a perfectly lovely beach and to potter around a bit on it, enjoying the views and looking at the plants, maybe sunning and swimming, too. 2. Gives you legitimate grounds for subsequently claiming that you were on a *hike* the whole time, so it's okay to stop for ice cream on the way back to the condo.

Driving instructions: Start as described in the driving instructions of Trip E20 Beyond Kihei, after you've gone briefly uphill and then past some big resorts, keep your eye on the signs pointing to beaches. Turn right where the sign points you seaward to Polo Beach, just over 17 miles from Wailuku. It's a block to the end of this short street, where you turn right into the parking lot for Polo Beach. The walkway to the beach is at the far end of the parking lot.

Permit/permission required: None.

Description: Descend the short flight of stairs to the beach and continue walking ahead to the black boulders at the north end of the beach. There's a splendid view of West Maui as you go. Several kinds of seaweed grow on just these few boulders; how many of them can you identify? (Sea lettuce was the only one I could identify.)

On the low, sandy bluff backing the beach, you'll find *akulikuli*, beach vitex (*pohinahina*), beach *naupaka* (*naupaka-kahakai*), and *ilima papa*—a nice little collection of naturally occurring plants for an area as developed as this one is. These plants are *indigenous* to Hawaii's beaches and to many other tropical Pacific coastlines, having arrived in Hawaii without human assistance. For example, the white fruits of beach *naupaka* are buoyant and tolerant of saltwater, so ocean currents can disperse them from one shoreline to another. According to *Hawaiian Coastal Plants and Scenic Shore-*

lines, development has taken a heavy toll on Hawaii's beach vitex plants, so it's good to see them flourishing here. *Kiawe* trees and tree heliotrope, both introduced species, grow atop the bluff.

It's only a few steps to the other end of the beach, where you can continue walking by stepping over trailing morning-glory vines and then crossing the black-pebble and white-coral beach of a little cove. A trail-of-use leads from here through *kiawe* to another pebbly cove that offers a fine view of Puu Olai, whose two summits are quite distinct from this vantage point. Out to sea, tiny Molokini lies in front of Kahoolawe, an island sacred in Hawaiian mythology—more about Kahoolawe below.

Return to the beach after taking in these fine views, and retrace your steps to your car when you're ready.

Kahoolawe. . . . Kahoolawe is too small and too arid to support a substantial population, but small family groups inhabited it well into historic times. It became a thriving cattle ranch in the first half of this century. One day after the Japanese attack on Pearl Harbor, the U.S. Navy seized Kahoolawe, dispossesed the ranch owners, and began using the island for target practice. After a long and bitter struggle between the U.S. Navy and Hawaiian groups determined to see the desecration stopped, Congress finally voted in 1990 to return Kahoolawe to Hawaii. Its restoration will be a fascinating project for those lucky enough to participate and an interesting story to follow for the rest of us.

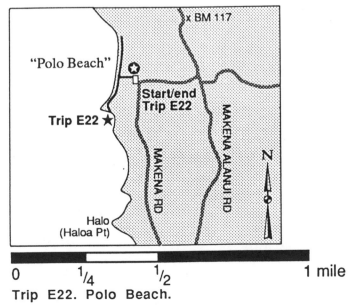

Trip E22. Polo Beach.

Trip E23. Kamaole County Beach Park 2 and 3

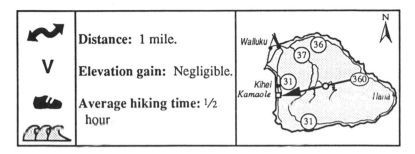

Distance: 1 mile.

Elevation gain: Negligible.

Average hiking time: ½ hour

Topos: Optional: *Puu o Kila* 7½.
Trail map (route approximated): At the end of this trip. There is no trail as such; you walk on the beach or on the grass as you please. Just how far *you* actually walk depends on whether you stick to the beach, detour to the grass, and so on.

Highlights: Views, picnic facilities, restrooms, a children's playground, plenty of sandy beach to stroll on and stretch out on, plenty of grass to move onto when that midday Kihei breeze picks up—Kamaole has lots to offer. There are 3 beaches in this park (Kamaole Beach County Parks 1, 2, and 3) separated by private property. Walking on the beach, you can circumvent the private property between 2 and 3 but not between 1 and 2: that's why I haven't included Kamaole 1 in this trip. This trip is better in the morning—you'll avoid the midday wind.

Driving instructions: Start as described in the driving instructions of Trip E20. In Kihei, keep your eyes peeled after you pass Kalama Beach County Park (seaward side) and Kihei Town Center (a shopping center). First you'll pass Kamaole 1, then some resorts and shopping malls, then Kamaole 2, and finally you'll reach Kamaole 3. Park near Kamaole 3 if possible (this trip starts at the south end of Kamaole 3) or Kamaole 2, 13–13⅓ miles from Wailuku, depending on where you park. If you come to a left-hand, uphill jog, you've gone too far; turn around.

Permit/permission required: None.

Description: Start your walk at the south end of Kamaole 3 (left end as you face the ocean). Stroll north (toward West Maui, looming in the distance) on the beach if the wind permits, on the grass if it doesn't. Kiawe, palms, and monkeypod trees shade the grass, where you'll also find tables, grills, restrooms, water, and playground equipment. At the north end of Kamaole 3, you'll need to be on the beach, or to detour to it, to circumvent a *kiawe*-covered point the top of which is marked PRIVATE PROPERTY. A trail-of-use along the low bluff below the point allows you to walk around to Kamaole 2 without trespassing. If tide and surf permit, you can walk out on the rocks here, exploring tidepools as you go—best not to do this barefooted!

Soon you're at the sandy south end of Kamaole 2, whose beach is somewhat longer. The pleasant grassy area of Kamaole 2 has no facilities but is brightened by morning glory, beach *naupaka*, autograph tree, and bougainvillea. As you stroll north, the grassy area ends where the buildings begin. The beach stretches farther in front of the buildings, but the path at the north end of the beach only leads up to private property. That's okay. Now that you've had a good look at Kamaole, it's time to make your really big decisions: where to stretch out in the sun, and whether to have your picnic lunch now or later. They're tough decisions when you have so many good choices. Maybe you should think it over as you amble back toward Kamaole 3, retracing your steps. In any case, you won't be in any hurry to get back to your car for a while. Enjoy your stay!

Kiawe tree and beach morning-glory, Maalaea Beach

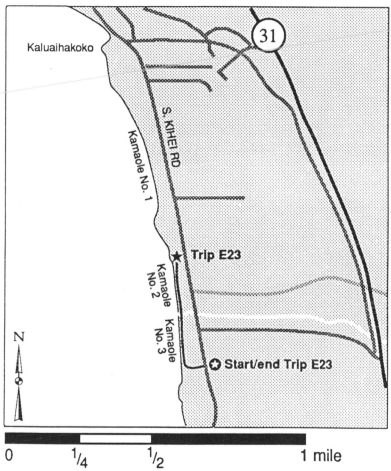

Trip E23. Kamaole County Beach Park 2 and 3.

Trip H1. Hosmer Grove Nature Loop

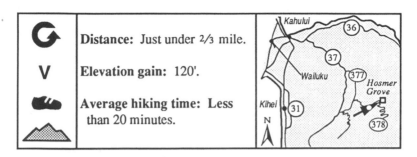

Distance: Just under ⅔ mile.

Elevation gain: 120'.

Average hiking time: Less than 20 minutes.

Topos: Optional: *Kilohana* 7½.

Trail map (route approximated): At the end of this trip.

Highlights: A number of native and introduced plants grow together here, and many of them are marked with numbered stakes so that you can identify them with the help of a brochure that should be available at the first numbered station. The brochure also has historical information and poses some intriguing questions about this area. It's a fine little hike even if the brochure isn't available. Birders should bring their binoculars and plan to take advantage of the bird-watching opportunities midway along the trail. Best in the early morning, as clouds and rain often move in by midmorning.

Driving instructions: From Wailuku, drive east on Highway 32 to its junction with Highway 36 (Hana Highway). Take Highway 36 to its junction with Highway 37 (Haleakala Highway). Take Highway 37 through Pukalani—last chance for gas and groceries—to the first junction with Highway 377. Turn left onto Highway 377, which is now the Haleakala Highway, and follow it through the green pasturelands of eucalyptus-shaded "upcountry" to its junction with Highway 378. Turn left onto Highway 378 (*it's* now the Haleakala Highway) and follow it uphill on its zigzagging course toward Haleakala's summit. Just after you cross the park boundary, a sign points left down a side road to Hosmer Grove and its campground, just under 30 miles from Wailuku. Turn left here and follow the side road past a spur road (to a radio facility) to the side road's end in ½ mile at the Hosmer Grove parking lot 30½ miles from Wailuku.

Cattle on the road are hazards drivers must watch out for. Many areas on the slopes along Highways 377 and 378 below the national park are pastures. There's no fence to keep the cattle that graze there from wandering onto the road, so of course they do. You're especially likely to find them on the road in the evening and at night. Be ready to stop for them. They'll amble off the road if you'll give them time.

Permit/permission required: None.

Description: Hosmer Grove, at 6800 feet, is not only high but potentially windy, cold, and wet. Be prepared with warm clothing that insulates when wet, with rain gear, and with shoes that will grip on slippery terrain. And take it easy if you're unaccustomed to hiking at higher altitudes!

Walk toward the trees, past the picnic pavilion, and pick up the path, paved at first, that leads away from the parking lot. As it bears north, you pass an information sign explaining that Hawaii's first territorial forester, Ralph S. Hosmer, planted this grove, now named in his honor, in 1910. The grove consists (like Polipoli) largely of continental species. Hosmer wanted to see if they would flourish here and support a timber industry. Fortunately, they didn't do well enough to compete with imported timber. As the pamphlet you'll pick up at the first station asks, "Do you think Haleakala would be a National Park today if the experiment had succeeded?"

You promptly cross a stream on a bridge. Exotic eucalyptuses dominate this first part of the grove. Red-berried *pukiawe*, a typical member of the native shrubland that is the natural cover of these slopes, struggles to survive beneath the huge, exotic trees. A procession of other exotics, beginning with sugi cedars, soon takes over from the eucalyptuses. The native shrubs beneath them are more interesting: *aalii, ohia lehua, mamane,* and more *pukiawe*.

Soon you reach an open spot where a bench overlooks a gully and an expanse of native shrubland slopes. Break out your binoculars and your bird-identification guides here and settle down for a look at native and exotic birds. When you move on, you're out of the grove proper and in native Hawaiian shrubland. A few seedlings of the exotic species may sprout here, but the Park Service is committed to pulling them up in order to allow the native plants to flourish. Otherwise, the naturally low native plants here would be shaded to death by the dense, towering exotics—as most of them have been in the grove you just left.

The Park Service must wage its fight in favor of native species and against exotics not only for plants but also for animals. The upper slopes of Haleakala are now completely fenced so that the Park Service can remove the non-native goats and pigs they find inside the fence with some confidence that another batch of goats and pigs won't immediately invade the park in their place. Inside the fence, native plants are recovering. However, a new threat confronts the park: rabbits have been appearing near the fence.

The trail soon curves back toward the campground. Near the end, false trails crisscross the main trail, but don't let them distract you. The trail returns to the end of the road you drove in on. Stay to picnic and enjoy the scenery!

Waikamoi Preserve. . . . The Nature Conservancy owns and manages Waikamoi Preserve, a native near-rainforest area next to Hosmer Grove. Waikamoi Preserve protects many rare and endangered native birds and plants. Birdwatching is the preserve's main attraction for the visitor. Access is by permit only, and travel is allowed on foot only.

The Nature Conservancy conducts guided hikes from Hosmer Grove into the preserve on a regular basis, currently the second Sunday of each month. Call the preserve manager at 1-808-572-7849 to reserve a place on their hike. You'll probably get a recording. I've been assured that the preserve manager does return all calls, but you will need to be within reach of your phone to catch that call.

The National Park Service also conducts "cloud forest" hikes in the preserve, currently on Monday, Thursday, and Friday mornings. Call the Park Service at 1-808-572-9306 to get the latest information. Reservations are not required. Once in a while, the hike may be canceled because of inclement weather, or for lack of a ranger to conduct the hike, or because too few people showed up (the hike requires a minimum of three people for safety). I recommend that you also call the Park Service the morning of the hike, as early as possible (they're in the office by 7 A.M.), to be sure it hasn't been canceled for either of the first two reasons. Hosmer Grove is probably hours away from where you're staying. There's a problem here: how can you get to Hosmer Grove in time for the hike without starting from your hotel well before 7 A.M.? You probably can't. Suggestion: take this book with you and drive toward Hosmer Grove but stop in, say, Pukalani for breakfast and call the Park Service around 7 A.M. from there. You'll still have time to get up to Hosmer Grove safely if the "cloud forest" hike is still on. Or, if it's been canceled, you'll have time to choose and take another hike.

You will need to make special arrangements directly with the preserve manager for any other access to Waikamoi Preserve.

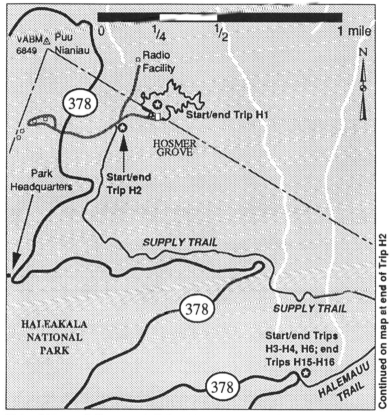

Trip H1 and Start of Trip H2. Hosmer Grove Nature Loop and Supply Trail.

Trip H2. Supply Trail to Crater Rim

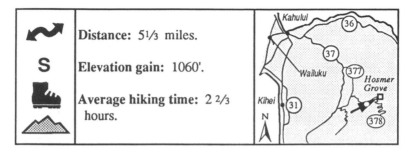

Distance: 5⅓ miles.

S

Elevation gain: 1060'.

Average hiking time: 2 ⅔ hours.

Kahului 36
37
Wailuku 377 *Hosmer Grove*
Kihei 31
N 378

Topos: *Kilohana* 7½.

Trail map: Begins on the map at the end of Trip H1; ends on the map at the end of this trip.

Highlights: This is the trail mule trains take to resupply the cabins in Haleakala's crater. For the hiker, it offers a close-up look at the native shrublands and breathtaking views downslope to East Maui's northeast coast (weather permitting) and, at its upper end, into the crater itself.

Driving instructions: Follow the driving instructions of Trip H1. Park at Hosmer Grove.

Permit/permission required: None.

Description: Walk back down the road you drove in on, past the spur road to the radio facility, 1/5 mile to the signed trailhead that will be on your left (south-southeast) in a wide, shallow, scrub-filled gully. Pick up the trail here and follow it uphill through *mamane, pukiawe, ohelo,* and *kukaenene*. Nearing ½ mile into this hike, the highway swings to the east and comes very close to the trail but is separated from it by a gully. You shortly cross a lava-floored gully just above a steep dropoff and pass a sign listing the park's rules (on your right). Alien, yellow-flowered evening primrose grows here; you'll see it far too often along the trails as well as along the roadside.

The trail bears east toward another gully, down whose steep, rocky sides water from seep springs drips. Just beyond ⅔ mile, you cross a section of flat, black lava, where rainwater may have pooled in the shallow depressions. Hosmer Grove and the radio facility are visible downhill to the north—convenient reference points. As the trail bears southeast, a highway bridge looms ahead to your right. The highway will be just above you, on your right, for a while. Do your best to ignore it as you make a brief, rocky descent, pass through a stone wall, and cross another section of lava. *Ohia lehua* trees grow here, leaning over the shallow pools in the rock. You meet a rather impressive pipeline and cross over it where it runs under the trail. At 1½ miles, just as it comes within yards of you, the highway switchbacks away from you at last. You cross a closed-off road (not shown on the map or the topo) and pick up the trail directly on the other side of it. You pass a rain shed ahead and some water tanks on your left.[1] On this last segment before you descend to the crater's rim, you'll want to pause often to take in the magnificent views down Haleakala's northeast slopes all the way to the sea, if the cloud cover permits. You cross intermittent streams, gullies, and a couple of culverts; a fern-lined intermittent streambed at 2 miles is especially pretty. Just beyond 2 miles, there's a meadowy area where the tramping of many feet and hooves has worn multiple tracks deep into the soft soil. Footing is spongy here.

You meet the Halemauu Trail at 2½ miles from your start, where a sign points you left to the CRATER. (On your way back, go right down the SUPPLY TRAIL at this junction.) Turn left onto the rocky Halemauu Trail, where *mamane* and a silvery, native shrub geranium line your route. You're descending now, and in a few steps you reach a gate in Haleakala's protective fence. Pass through the gate, being sure it closes behind you. A couple of switchbacks bring you down to a sweeping crater view just before the trail makes a third switchback. This is your destination for this hike. Find a perch here where you can spend some time to watch the show. On your left, Koolau Gap opens. Clouds often fill it, drifting across the crater floor. Shifting clouds may reveal a feature for a moment, then hide it again while parting to show another feature. The green, spire-studded cliffs of Leleiwi *Pali* (*pali* means cliffs) fall steeply away at your feet to a meadow that's more than a thousand feet below. On your left, the Halemauu Trail snakes down, down, down the steep ridge that juts into the crater, and the crater walls rise again across Koolau Gap. Eastward, fantastically colored cinder cones dot the crater floor.

It's hard to leave this awesome sight, but you can console yourself with more of those fine views toward the coast as you retrace your steps back to Hosmer Grove.

Crater trips overview. . . . Visualizing the crater's trail system can be difficult, especially as you're taking your first look at it over the crater rim. It's helpful to think of the network of maintained trails in Haleakala's crater as forming a sloppy letter Y,

---

[1] The topo shows a rain shed and water tanks on your right (west), but they are now on your left (east).

knocked over onto its left side, with a crooked tail, as shown in the not-to-scale drawing below. One arm of the **Y** starts at the trailhead for the Halemauu Trail. The other arm of the **Y** starts at the trailhead for the Sliding Sands Trail. There are a couple of maintained spur trails, and there are three maintained interconnecting trails between the Sliding Sands and the Halemauu trails in the vicinity of the Bottomless Pit. The Sliding Sands and the Halemauu trails meet not far from Paliku Cabin/Campground to begin the tail of the **Y**. Just past Paliku Cabin/Campground, the tail turns almost 90x south toward Kaupo village.

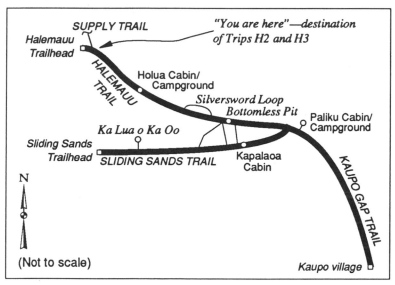

Visualizing the Crater Trails

The trips in this book describe a variety of dayhikes and backpacks in Haleakala's crater covering the current network of *maintained* trails. There's a trip to each of the cabins/campgrounds and a unique dayhike from each cabin/campground. See Appendix A for information on permits and cabin reservations. See the note following Trip H4 for the importance of staying on the *maintained* trails.

Dayhikes from the crater's rim. Trips H4, H10, H11, H12, and H15 are dayhikes from the crater's rim. The most comprehensive trip is strenuous Trip H15 down the Sliding Sands Trail, through the crater, and out on the Halemauu Trail (requires a car shuttle). It's one of the best hikes in this book and on Maui.

A note on the Sliding Sands Trail. Some people consider the Sliding Sands Trail to be too difficult to hike out on because of its "loose" surface. However, hikers in good shape may not agree. The surface has been consolidated to some extent by years of being hiked on; that's certainly the way I found it. My friend Ray Brouillard, who backpacked in and out on the Sliding Sands Trail, reports that he had no problem hiking out. Others report similar experiences. The bottom line: if you're fit, don't let the reputation of the Sliding Sands Trail deter you!

To Holua Cabin/Campground. Trip H4, which you can make as either a dayhike or a backpack, takes you to Holua Cabin/Campground in the northwest corner of the crater. Trip H4 is teamed with Trip H5, which is a dayhike from Holua Cabin/Campground to Kapalaoa Cabin.

To Kapalaoa Cabin. Trip H12, which you can make as either a dayhike or a backpack, takes you to Kapalaoa Cabin. Trip H12 is teamed with Trip H13, which is a dayhike from Kapalaoa Cabin to Holua Cabin/Campground via a somewhat different route from that taken by Trip H5. Or you can reverse part of Trip H5 to make it a dayhike from Kapalaoa Cabin.

To Paliku Cabin/Campground. Trip H6 builds on Trip H4 to take you down the Halemauu Trail from Holua Cabin/Campground to Paliku Cabin/Campground. Trip H6 is teamed with Trip H7, which is a dayhike from Paliku Cabin/Campground down Kaupo Gap to the park's boundary. Trip H7 thus complements Trip E16, which is a dayhike from Kaupo village up Kaupo Gap to the park's boundary. Trip H14 takes you down the Sliding Sands Trail to Paliku Cabin/Campground with an optional night at Kapalaoa Cabin. It's certainly feasible for the sturdier hiker to backpack all the way to Paliku in one day from either the Halemauu or Sliding Sands trailhead because it's mostly downhill. The trip out—uphill—will be more enjoyable if you stay the night at Holua Cabin/Campground or Kapalaoa Cabin.

The grand crater tour. Trip H16 is "the grand crater tour." You visit each cabin or cabin/campground on a three-night shuttle trip between the Sliding Sands and the Halemauu trailheads. Sturdy early-birds will be able to make morning dayhikes on some of the other crater trails from Holua Cabin/Campground or from Kapalaoa Cabin (e.g., Trips H5 and H13) and still hike out of the crater in the afternoon.

Kaupo Gap. The backpack from either the Sliding Sands or the Halemauu trailhead all the way across the crater floor and down Kaupo Gap to Kaupo village requires an extremely long shuttle. Most visitors will find that shuttle to be very difficult to arrange. You may not camp beyond Paliku Cabin/Campground, and there is no readily available water along the way, not even in Kaupo village. Also, the layout of the crater trails and the short time you're allowed to stay in the crater (3 nights maximum in any 30-day period) means you'll have to choose between the Halemauu and Sliding Sands trails. It's just not practical to see the entire crater *and* hike out down Kaupo Gap. That's why I treated Kaupo Gap in two trips, Trip E16 from Kaupo village up to the park boundary, and Trip H7, a side trip from Paliku Cabin down to the park boundary. You won't need a shuttle, and you'll have more time to enjoy the crater or Kaupo Gap or both.

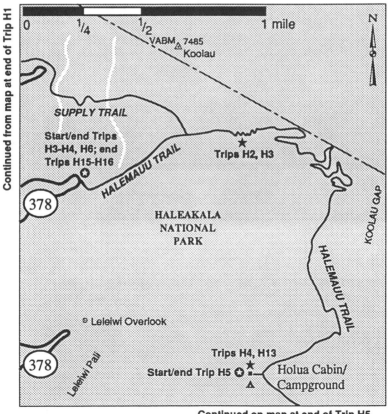

Continued on map at end of Trip H5

Trips H3-H4 and Start of Trip H6. Halemauu Trailhead.

Trip H3. Halemauu Trail to Crater Rim

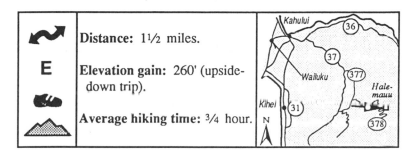

Distance: 1½ miles.

E

Elevation gain: 260' (upside-down trip).

Average hiking time: ¾ hour.

Topos: *Kilohana* 7½.

Trail map: At the end of Trip H2.

Highlights: The spectacular view down into Haleakala's crater is the main attraction on this short hike.

Driving instructions: Follow the driving instructions of Trip H1 but don't turn off at the side road to Hosmer Grove. Instead, continue up Highway 378 toward the Visitor Center, a little over ¾ mile farther. It's a good idea to stop here for information and to get any books and maps you may need. (Topos are *not* available there or anywhere else on Maui as of this writing.) Back on the road, it's a little less than 3½ more miles to the turnoff to the parking lot for the Halemauu Trail, 34¼ miles from Wailuku.

Several *nene,* the endangered native goose that is the state bird of Hawaii, frequent the Halemauu Trail's parking lot. Your start is apt to be delayed while you enjoy their antics and take some pictures of them. See below for more about the nene.

Permit/permission required: None.

Description: The start of the Halemauu Trail is a little deceptive: you'd expect it to lead straight away from the parking lot east toward the crater rim. But in fact, it starts off southeastward, passes an information sign where you may find brochures on the park, and finally angles northeast at a little gully. (Remember this for your return.) Descending gently, you contour briefly around Haleakala's slopes through native shrubland. Yellow-flowered *mamane,* red-berried *ohelo,* and a white-flowered native shrub geranium add interest to the trail. If the weather permits, you'll have some fine views downslope all the way to the ocean, some 7700 feet below and many miles away.

As you near the ⅔-mile point, you meet the supply trail from Hosmer Grove (Trip H2). From here, you continue ahead on the

Halemauu Trail through the gate to the crater-rim viewpoint as described in Trip H2, just under ¾ mile from your start. When you can tear yourself away, retrace your steps.

Nene. . . . This handsome, non-migratory goose is believed to have descended from the migratory Brant and Canada geese that occasionally winter over in the Hawaiian Islands. Unlike their ancestors, the *nene* aren't waterfowl. One of the *nene*'s adaptations to this dry habitat is feet that are only partially webbed.

There were once as many as 25,000 *nene* in the islands. But by the early 1950s, it was estimated that there were only 30 wild *nene* left. Their habitat had been destroyed by the deforestation that had left so much of Hawaii stripped of her native trees. Introduced animals, particularly mongooses and cats, had destroyed *nene* eggs, chicks, and nesting adults. Concerted efforts in Hawaii and in England have enabled the *nene* to survive in captivity. *Nene* have been reintroduced into the wild here at Haleakala National Park, on the Big Island at Hawaii Volcanoes National Park, and on Kauai in the lowlands around Lihue. It's not known whether they can successfully reestablish themselves in the wild, because the introduced animals that prey on them haven't been controlled.

Nene "honk" like other geese, but you're more likely to hear another of their calls, a cow-like "moo." Here at Haleakala, they are filling a sort of ecological niche, but in their own *nene* style. On the mainland, the campground beggars are typically ground squirrels, bluejays, and raccoons—the latter two are out-and-out thieves. Haleakala's *nene* aren't thieves, but they're accomplished beggars. They come running, literally, when you drive up and open a car door, set out a picnic cooler, unzip a daypack, or pull some trail mix out of your pocket. You must be hardhearted and not feed them. (It's both the law and common sense, so they won't become dependent on people supplying food.) However, you will probably feel as guilty as I do when one of them stands there in front of you, eyeing your sandwich hopefully and mooing as if to say, "I'm endangered, I'm adorable, *feed me!*" Just hang onto your goodies. You'll be off the hook as soon as someone else drives up and opens a car door, sets out a picnic cooler, ...

Trip H4. Halemauu Trail to Holua Cabin Dayhike or Backpack

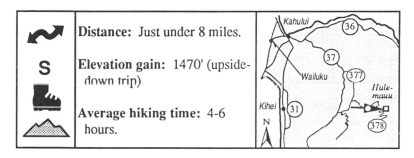

Distance: Just under 8 miles.

Elevation gain: 1470' (upside-down trip).

Average hiking time: 4-6 hours.

Topos: *Kilohana* 7½.

Trail map: At the end of Trip H2.

Highlights: The awesome view from the Halemauu Trail at the crater rim, which is the destination of Trips H2 and H3, is just the beginning of *this* breathtaking scenic adventure down into the northwest corner of Haleakala's crater. This trail is so beautiful and so well-engineered that the return trip uphill can be as enjoyable as the descent if you take the time to appreciate it. While it's described below as a dayhike, you can also do it as a backpack if you can get permission to stay at Holua Cabin or the adjacent campground.

Driving instructions: Follow the driving instructions of Trip H3.

Permit/permission required: None for a dayhike. Required for an overnight stay at Holua Cabin (by reservation only) or at the adjacent campground; see Appendix A.

Description: Follow Trip H3 to the crater rim and take in the view. Now continue your zigzagging way down the Halemauu Trail, sometimes indistinct here because of multiple crossing tracks. Watch your step if it's been raining, as these rocks can be very slippery. It's not long before you cross a narrow saddle where, if the cloud-cover permits, you have dizzying views into the crater on your right and down Haleakala's green northern slopes to the sea on your left—one of the very best viewpoints on this or any other hike in this book!

Soon you're negotiating carefully engineered switchbacks as you descend Leleiwi *Pali* to the crater floor. The grade is moderate to gentle, and the views are always spectacular. Stop often to enjoy them! One long switchback carries you around the other side of this ridge for a look down Koolau Gap. Seep springs dampen the black rock of the *pali*, which provides a perfect backdrop for the jewellike colors of the *amauu* fern. Mature *amauu* fronds are a bright green, while young fronds are a bright red. Together, set against the black rock, they're a sight you'll never forget. The red pigment is said to protect young fronds against the intense radiation at these altitudes.

You reach the crater floor at a stock gate in a little less than 3 miles from your start. Pass through the fence and please close the gate behind you. You may have expected to be on a dry, cinder-covered crater floor like the ones you see in most photographs of the crater. But here, the crater floor is a broad meadow of tall, waving grasses, nourished by the moisture in the clouds that flow through Koolau Gap. The trail is sometimes hard to see in the high growth, so watch your step and beware of half-hidden rocks. Bizarre, twisted peaks of half-vegetated lava rock rise out of the meadow here and there.

Holua Cabin sits atop a plateau on the opposite (south) side of this meadow. Follow the trail across the meadow, on the other side of which the trail rises gradually up the lava plateau in a few lazy switchbacks. You reach a T-junction atop the plateau, just under 4 miles from your start. The Halemauu Trail turns sharply left (southeast) here toward the Silversword Loop, the Bottomless Pit, and Paliku Cabin. You turn right to Holua Cabin, which is just a few steps away, sitting on a tidy, grassy flat. There's water, a picnic table, a toilet, and a few semi-resident nene here. If you're staying the night in the campground, it's 120 feet farther up the plateau on a short, steep spur trail that goes off to the left, past the water tap, as you face the cabin.

Return the way you came.

Crater trails. . . . The system of *maintained* trails leading down into and through the crater follows routes through this delicate ecosystem that are safe for you and for the environment. Going off the maintained trails can be physically hazardous and can damage the ecosystem, particularly in the extremely sensitive western part of the crater. Please don't step off the trail even to photograph the silverswords. You could be trampling and killing tiny silversword sprouts you can't even see. You'll find silverswords growing right next to the trail in several places, especially on the spur trail to Ka Lua o Ka Oo (Trip H11), so stepping off the trail is unnecessary. There aren't as many maintained trails as there used to be, "thanks" to cuts in the funding for national parks. But trust me on this: there's more than enough to explore on the remaining *maintained* trails to keep you busy for the few days you're permitted to spend in the crater. Haleakala National Park hopes to start maintaining more trails and to reopen closed ones over the next few years. Stick to the maintained trails, spare the environment, spare yourself injury, and help keep Haleakala beautiful.

Haleakala Crater seen from the Visitor Center

Trip H5. Holua Cabin/Campground Side Trip to Kapalaoa Cabin

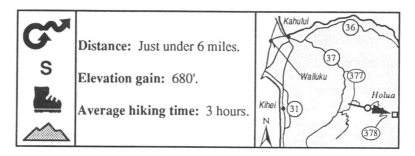

Distance: Just under 6 miles.

Elevation gain: 680'.

Average hiking time: 3 hours.

Topos: *Kilohana,* Nahiku 7½.
Trail map: At the end of this trip.
Highlights: This delightful semiloop takes you to the famous Silversword Loop and through some of the most colorful volcanic areas in the crater. It's one of several dayhikes you might take while staying at Holua Cabin/ Campground. See the note at the end of Trip H2 for more ideas on crater dayhikes and backpacks.
Driving instructions: Not applicable.
Permit/permission required: None for the side trip, which is a dayhike. Required to stay at Holua Cabin or the adjacent campground (see Trip H4 and Appendix A).
Description: Trip H4 has gotten you to Holua Cabin. This trip starts from the T-junction in front of Holua Cabin and bears southeast on the Halemauu Trail. You ascend gradually past a pit that is the open mouth of a lava tube and then through low ridges of jagged brown lava whose outcrops are crusted with a white lichen and whose protected hollows hold plants. At first you'll see *mamane, aalii,* sword ferns, and bracken ferns. But soon the terrain becomes drier, and *ohelo, pilo, pukiawe, kukaenene,* dubautias, and even a few silverswords appear. Lava cinders crunch under your boots. On either side of the trail, islands of fantastically shaped lava twist and twirl up from beds of black and red cinder. Sometimes the clouds from Koolau Gap drift in, leaving you alone in a misty world of goblin forms. At other times, you can see far across the crater to the cliffs enclosing it and to the red, brown, and black cinder cones that dot its floor. Pause often to look around you. It's one of earth's most striking landscapes, often referred to as a moonscape.
    One mile from Holua, you reach the first of two junctions with the famous Silversword Loop. It's less a loop than a ¼-mile diver-

sion from the Halemauu Trail. Veer left onto the Silversword Loop at this first junction for just over ¼ mile and then rejoin the main trail. When you've been around the Silversword Loop and come back to the Halemauu Trail, turn left to continue south on this dayhike.

Back on the Halemauu Trail, you descend briefly on soft, fine sand and walk through a red-tinged Mars-scape of bizarre lava rocks. Cinder cones rise on either side of the trail, and you soon reach another junction, just under 2 miles from your start at Holua Cabin/Campground. Both the left and the right forks here will get you to Kapalaoa Cabin and the Sliding Sands Trail, but take the left fork east toward the Bottomless Pit for now. As you approach the Bottomless Pit, you see a natural, if somewhat sloppy, bull's-eye of soft reds, grays, golds, and oranges ahead on the southeast slope of an unnamed cone. The slopes are a deep red with dots of fiery red and a brilliant splash of gold and orange at the saddle with Halalii conc. Orange, red, and lavender along the trail contrast with the dark brown slopes to your left, while on your right, pinks, golds, and reds spill into Halalii cone's vent. A lively brick red splashes up one slope, vivid orange another; nearby, there's a pit of shattered gray and red-brown rock. Grasses and dubautia make their homes here, adding a dash of green. Now you know why this area is referred to as "Pele's Paint Pot." No subdued watercolors here—these are bold tempera colors, the result of minerals in the volcanic rock. Sulfur compounds are responsible for the yellows, iron for the reds. The fenced-off Bottomless Pit is not bottomless; according to a sign, it's 65 feet deep. Its depth may be forgettable, but its colors are memorable: pinks and reds burst from its throat; golds and grays tint its edges. Ignore the unmarked side trail that leads south away from the Bottomless Pit (it's just a shortcut over the saddle between Halalii and Puu Naue to the trail you'll be returning on). Instead, continue generally eastward around Puu Naue, past brown-black cinder cones whose slopes are daubed with patches of orange and red. Ahead looms Puu Mamane, its northern slopes green with vegetation, its southern slopes bare red cinders. Now you pass through a cinder-strewn landscape as desolate as any you've seen; silverswords grow high on the slopes to your right. Soon, the bare, reddish cone of Puu Nole rises ahead on your right, Puu Mamane on your left. You pass a couple of trails-of-use down which you have views of Kapalaoa Cabin. At the next marked junction, between Puu Mamane and Puu Nole, you turn southeast (right) toward Kapalaoa Cabin on the easternmost Sliding Sands-Halemauu spur trail. The green-clad *pali* behind the cabin dominate the scenery as you begin a descent between Puu

Naue and Puu Nole. As you approach the red slopes of another cone, you see that they have a sparse cover of bracken fern and silversword. A group of silverswords grows where the trail brushes past a ridge extending from the cone. Jagged chunks of rock protrude through the sand here, looking like the spine of a prehistoric monster half-buried in the sand. You level out on black sand that's tinged with lavender and strewn with red and orange cinders; soon you reach a junction with the Sliding Sands Trail. Turn *left* (east) here for a few steps to Kapalaoa Cabin, 1¼ mile from the Bottomless Pit. Here you'll find a toilet, a picnic table, water, and nene anxious to help you polish off that granola bar. There's no tent-campground here: water at Kapalaoa Cabin is limited to precipitation collected from the roof, and there's not enough to support both a cabin and a campground.

The trail that goes north immediately in front of Kapalaoa Cabin is not a maintained trail, so you go west ⅓ mile, past the junction with the trail you descended on, to the next marked trail junction. Turn right (northwest) here onto the middle Sliding Sands-Halemauu spur trail toward Holua Cabin. You head toward Puu Naue through bunches of a native alpine tussock grass—a sort of meadow and just about the last thing you'd expect to see in this lava wilderness. The grass ends as you pass a red-cinder hillock, and you traverse a region of black and reddish sand and of lava frozen as it oozed across the landscape. The rocks here are riddled with holes left by gas bubbles and brushed with subtle hues from cream through orange, red, and black. You cross a spine of lava, climb past a miniature butte of red rock, and level out amid reddish cinders and black boulders. A remnant of a *pahoehoe* flow, markedly smoother than the *aa* you've been passing, appears on your left. The trail is plain ahead of you, winding up to the saddle between Ka Moa o Pele and Halalii cones. Ka Moa o Pele's huge red vent gapes at you, its edges dusted with ochre and gray. You pass more *pahoehoe*, cross a stretch of black cinders, and abruptly enter a region of light-colored cinders—white, tan, pink-orange—on which sit isolated lava bombs. The light-colored cinders end as abruptly as they began, and you're soon on the saddle between Ka Moa o Pele and Halalii cones at the junction with the spur trail around Halalii, a little under 1 mile from Kapalaoa Cabin. Head northwest (right) past a little, squarish vent called Pele's Pig Pen to the junction where, earlier, you turned off to the Bottomless Pit.

Bear left (northwest) on the Halemauu Trail here and retrace your steps to Holua Cabin to end this beautiful dayhike.

Continued from map at end of Trip H2

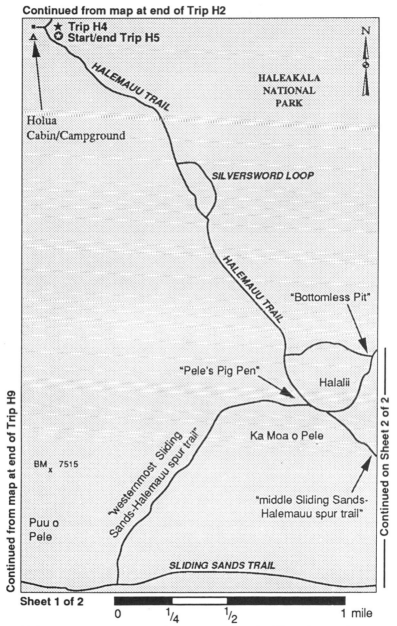

Trips H5 and H13; Trips H12-H16 (Continued).
Halemauu and Sliding Sands Trails to/from Kapalaoa
(Sheet 1 of 2).

168   MAUI TRAILS

Continued on map at end of Trip H6

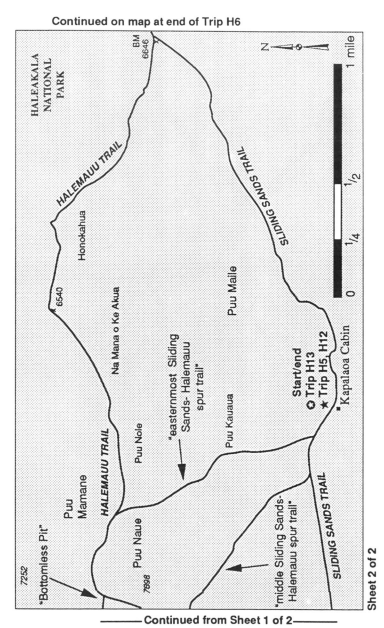

Sheet 2 of 2

Continued from Sheet 1 of 2

Trips H5 and H13; Trips H12-H16 (Continued). Halemauu and Sliding Sands Trails to/from Kapalaoa (Sheet 2 of 2).

Trip H6. Halemauu Trail
to Paliku Cabin/Campground Backpack

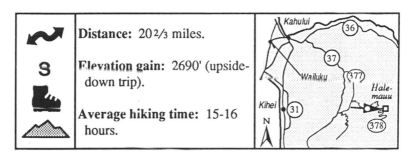

Distance: 20 2/3 miles.

Elevation gain: 2690' (upside-down trip).

Average hiking time: 15-16 hours.

Topos: *Kilohana, Nahiku* 7½.

Trail map: Begins on the map at the end of Trip H4; continues on the map at the end of Trip H5; ends on the map at the end of this trip.

Highlights: The soft, green beauty of the *pali* and meadows near Holua Cabin/Campground and around Paliku Cabin/Campground contrast marvelously with the vivid mineral colors and harsh aridity of the crater backcountry that separates them.

Driving instructions: Follow the driving instructions of Trip H3.

Permit/permission required: Haleakala National Park permit required to stay overnight at Holua Cabin/Campground or Paliku Cabin/Campground or both. See "Getting Permits and Permission" and Appendix A.

Description: You can organize this trip in a number of different ways depending on the permits you're able to get and whether you want to take a layover day. Clearly, going all the way to Paliku in one day and all the way out in one day is the most strenuous version. I've described an easier version below: you go all the way to Paliku in one day—mostly downhill—and take two days to walk out, staying one night at Holua Cabin/Campground.

Day 1 (10⅓ miles). Follow Trip H4 to Holua Cabin/Campground. From there, follow Trip H5 to the marked junction between Puu Mamane and Puu Nole, where Trip H5 turns right (southeast) toward Kapalaoa Cabin. Bear left (ahead; east) toward Paliku Cabin/Campground at that junction. You presently reach a saddle where a low, vegetated hill rises ahead of you. As you continue, the cliffs around the crater begin to assume a softer, greener look. Soon you're gazing across an almost-African landscape, where the *veldt* is shrubs and bracken rather than grass, dotted by green *kopjes* whose tops sport tree-sized mamane rather than the airy African acacia. You descend gradually onto the *veldt,* and you presently see what looks like a dry wash ahead. It is a wash, and the trail leads down to it. In some places, the trail is right in the wash; in others, where the bottom of the wash is very rocky, the trail leads you around its edges.

At the foot of shrub-covered Oili Puu, you reach the junction of the Halemauu and Sliding Sands trails. Turn left (northeast) here toward Paliku Cabin/Campground, abandoning the wash and following a path sometimes over pahoehoe and sometimes worn deeply through the shrub-and-bracken plain. The troughs of the grey-black pahoehoe ripples are sometimes highlighted by a delicate trace of red color.

At a junction with the trail heading down Kaupo Gap, you can just glimpse Paliku Cabin to the northeast. It's surrounded by trees and nestled at the foot of lushly green *pali,* sometimes framed in a rainbow by late-afternoon light refracted through a fine rain. Bear left (northeast) on the side trail ¼ mile to Paliku Cabin/Campground, 6⅓ miles from Holua Cabin/Campground. The spur trail to the campground is on your left a few dozen yards before you get to Paliku Cabin. Nene patrol the picnic area in front of the cabin and the adjacent campground, mooing for a handout. Not far from Paliku cabin, there's a rangers' cabin (almost hidden) and a meadow where horses graze. It's a lovely place to stay, and you'll probably want to spend two nights here in order to take Trip H7.

Day 2 (6⅓ miles). Reverse your steps from Paliku Cabin/ Campground to Holua Cabin/Campground.

Day 3 (Just under 4 miles). Reverse your steps from Holua Cabin/Campground to the Halemauu trailhead.

Why the great variations in the amount of vegetation? ... You'll no doubt have noticed the great variation in the amount of vegetation in the crater. What a contrast the arid volcanic landscapes around the Silversword Loop and the Bottomless Pit make with the meadows around Holua Cabin/Campground and Paliku Cabin/Campground! One factor is the difference in precipitation the different parts of the crater receive. In general, the crater floor near Koolau Gap (Holua Cabin/Campground and the meadow) shares the moisture of East Maui's rainy northern coast, which flows through Koolau Gap. The crater floor here is just within the inversion-layer zone. Above Paliku Cabin/Campground, there's a notch in the slim ridge still separating Kipahulu Valley from Kaupo Gap and Haleakala's crater. Moisture from the very wet Hana-

Kipahulu coast pours through this notch, nourishing Paliku. By contrast, the southwest edge of the crater is on the dry, leeward side of the island and is high above the inversion-layer zone. Annual rainfall in the crater varies from 20 inches there to 200 or more inches at Paliku!

But rainfall variations alone aren't enough to explain the differences. An annual rainfall of 20 inches a year is more than enough to sustain a cover of vegetation in many areas of the world. However, in order for that vegetation to flourish, the soil must retain the water it receives. The crater's cinder cones, remnants of its last phase of volcanic activity, have made the crater both a visual delight and an inhospitable desert. Their eruptions covered most of the crater with a porous layer of cinder and ash, reported to be 3000 feet deep in some places. That layer allows whatever precipitation falls to percolate right through it. Little water is retained, except in isolated pockets, to feed plants. Nooks like Paliku escaped those cinders. Unlike the cinder deserts, their older, more consolidated soils retain life-giving water and create these green oases.

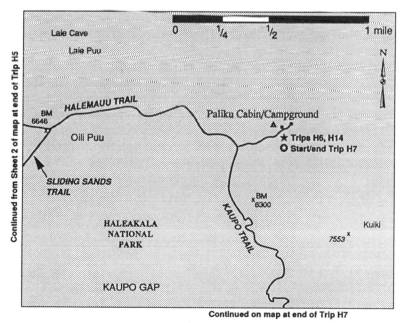

Continued on map at end of Trip H7

Trips H6 and H14 (End) and Start of Trip H7.
Halemauu and Sliding Sands Trails to Paliku.

Trip H7. Paliku Cabin/Campground Side Trip to Park Boundary

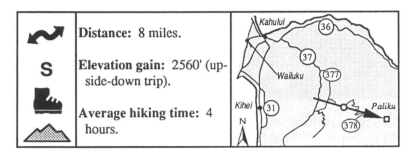

Distance: 8 miles.

Elevation gain: 2560' (up-side-down trip).

Average hiking time: 4 hours.

Topos: *Nahiku, Kaupo 7½.*

Trail map: Begins on the map at the end of Trip H6; ends on the map at the end of this trip.

Highlights: A fascinating descent through scrubland, forest, and meadow, with fine views downslope to the coast around Kaupo village. This trip complements Trip E16.

Driving instructions: Not applicable.

Permit/permission required: None just for this side trip, but you must have permission to stay in the crater as described in Trips H4 and H6.

Description: Trip H6 or H14 brought you to Paliku Cabin/Campground. To begin this trip, retrace your steps from Paliku Cabin/Campground to the junction with the trail that goes down Kaupo Gap. Turn left (southwest) toward the dark peak, Haleakala, that guards the west side of Kaupo Gap. (Haleakala peak is too far south and west of the trail to appear on the book's maps.) Opposite, Kuiki peak watches Kaupo Gap's east side. The trail presently veers south and begins a descent on a cindery surface through the scrub you've come to recognize as typical of this region. Look for some almost-tree-sized *aalii* shrubs here. In ½ mile from Paliku, you begin a series of cinder-covered switchbacks. White-flowered *ulei* grows here, as do many splendid amauu ferns. Down you go, leveling out in a little forest, then emerging into a meadow of waving grasses through which you follow the trail to the edge of this bench. Here, you may be startled to realize that the blue vastness ahead of you is only half sky. The lower portion is the sparkling ocean, so far away that it blends into the sky.

You switchback briefly down to another bench and another

meadow. From here, you make a delightful descent over an old, built-up trail whose supporting lava-rock walls are covered with a thick white fluff of lichens. Spikes of small, blue-flowered vervain sway along the trailside. Now you reach a third bench, pushing your way first through blackberry and then through dense grass. The sheer walls of Kaupo Gap loom high on your left.

Rounding a curve, you find yourself walking south along the west side of a gully whose shady east side is well-clothed in native plants, including *ohia* trees, *amauu* ferns, and *mamane* shrubs. As you veer west and then south, the view opens up again, and you see some fine *koa* trees down in the gully. On the rocks to your right, look for the low, trailing kukaenene with its shiny black berries.

The next series of switchbacks offers breathtaking views down to Kaupo and the sea, west to Haleakala peak, and back up to the misty *pali*. The trail becomes very rocky, and with so many loose rocks, it's wise to pause when you want to enjoy the scenery. You leave the rocks at a little clearing in the now-predominant *koa*. The terrain has become drier as you have descended, as you can see from the shrubbier forms of the *mamane* and *pukiawe*. Soon the trail becomes rocky again, and you resume descending on switchbacks under the shade of *koa* trees. At a little emerald meadow, pause to check the gentle slope ahead and slightly to your right (south-southwest) to see where the trail resumes, as it all but vanishes in the lush grass here. Make your way across the meadow and pick up the trail again as it rises briefly on the low ridge, then follows the ridge generally south through scrub, becoming quite rocky and sometimes steep. Soon you begin a series of grassy switchbacks that bring you to the protective fence of the Kaupo Gap Study Area.

Now you descend moderately on a track that's more often grass than rock. The slopes ahead of you frame distant, square-shaped Kamanawa Bay west of Kaupo village. At an apparent fork, either fork will do, but watch your footing on the deep grass. It makes a spongy surface to walk on and conceals some loose rocks. You pass a National Park boundary sign on the other side of which is a sign announcing that you're now on Kaupo Ranch's private property. Soon you cross a gully above some *koa* trees and, as the track grows faint, duck into a lovely grove of *koa* just before the park's protective boundary fence. Remember that if you do go through the fence, you must be sure the gate shuts securely behind you, even if you have to trample the grass down to make it close.

Retrace your steps to Paliku Cabin/Campground when you're ready. (To continue to Kaupo, reverse the steps of Trip E16.)

Maui and Haleakala peak. . . . Shelters, platforms, and a *heiau* are said to be located on Haleakala peak, signs that it once had religious significance. One source speculates that Haleakala peak may be the site of the demigod Maui's mythical encounter with La, the sun. There are many versions of this myth, but all agree that long ago, the lazy sun moved across the sky so quickly that the day was very short. La arose from his resting-place reluctantly, hurried as fast as he could through his work of lighting and warming the earth, and rushed home to his leisure without a thought for the long nights that people had to endure. The day was far too short for Maui's mother, the goddess Hina, to dry her *kapa,* the bark cloth characteristic of Polynesia. Hina asked Maui to find a way to dry her *kapa.* Here on Hale-a-ka-La, the House of the Sun, Maui prepared ropes and hid so he could surprise La as he rose, climbing over the walls of Haleakala crater like a spider, one leg—ray—at a time. As La put each leg over the *pali,* Maui lassoed it. He held La captive until La promised to move across the sky more slowly. Even then, some accounts say, Maui left a few of the ropes on La's legs. You can see them trailing off into the sky just before the sun sets.

The island of Maui is unique in Polynesia: it is the only island named for a deity. Maui was a great mischief-maker, and legends about his escapades (or "strifes") occur throughout Polynesia. Martha Beckwith reported in *Hawaiian Mythology* that Maui legends in Hawaii tend to be "minutely localized." East Maui, West Maui, the Big Island of Hawaii, Oahu, and Kauai all have their own versions of the same Maui exploit, placing the exploit's location somewhere on that island. For East Maui, Maui's tricks usually occur near Kauiki at Hana; for West Maui, near Kahakuloa. Haleakala *isn't* one of the sites Dr. Beckwith records in association with Maui's legends. Still, legends are fluid, and Haleakala certainly seems appropriate as a poetic, if not entirely traditional, site for Maui's capture of La.

Continued from map at end of Trip H6

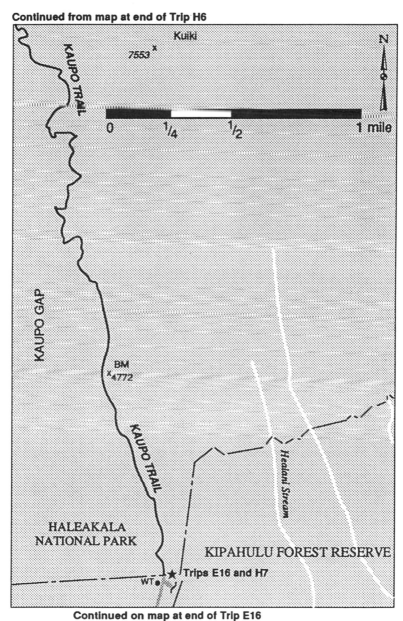

Continued on map at end of Trip E16

Trips E16, H7. Kaupo Trail.

Trip H8. Kalahaku Overlook Miniloop

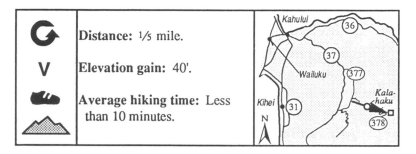

Distance: ⅕ mile.

Elevation gain: 40'.

Average hiking time: Less than 10 minutes.

Topos: Optional: *Kilohana* 7½.
    Trail map: At the end of this trip.
    Highlights: This brief trip offers you fine crater views and a visit to a little garden of silverswords in just a few brief minutes of walking with little elevation gain. Non-hikers, this is the Haleakala hike for *you!*
    Driving instructions: Follow the driving instructions of Trip H4 past the Halemauu Trail turnoff. Continue up the highway to the Visitor Center at White Hill, 40⅓ miles from Wailuku, *deliberately driving past the turnoff for the Kalahaku Overlook*—all but invisible when driving up the highway. You're not allowed to turn off here when you're going uphill. Turn around in the parking lot at the Visitor Center and drive back *down* the highway just over 1½ miles to the turnoff for the Kalahaku Overlook, well-marked for downhill traffic. Turn right here and follow the spur road to the parking area, 42 miles from Wailuku. (It's 38¾ miles from Wailuku plus the slightly over 3 miles you drove to the Visitor Center and back.)
    Permit/permission required: None.
    Description: Near the end of the spur road, a paved path leads up to an overlook shelter. Taking this path, you climb with the help of some stairs past a sign explaining the impact non-native animals have had on native plants and animals. Don't take the path that branches to the right at a junction here; instead, continue ahead to the shelter on the crater rim. There's a magnificent crater view from the shelter, and interpretive signs explain the many crater cones you can see below to the east and southeast. To the west, you can see West Maui.
    It's hard to leave this view, but when you're ready, retrace your steps to the exotic-animal sign. Turn left at the junction here and follow the paved path down a gentle descent with a short flight of stairs

to the road. Cross the road and descend the stairs that are just a little to your right. Turn left at the bottom of the stairs and follow the paved path along the silversword viewing area. You can't walk out into the silversword garden, but you can walk back and forth here to see how the light brings out the silvery patina on these remarkable plants.

The path winds back up to the road, where you turn left (north) and retrace your steps to your car.

The Brocken specter. . . . is a natural light show in which you are both audience and star: your shadow on a cloud bank below you, surrounded by a rainbow ring. It's often seen at Haleakala, particularly from Leleiwi *Pali* (for example, Leleiwi Overlook, just down the highway). Afternoon sunlight behind you casts your shadow onto the clouds drifting through Koolau Gap. The light around your shadow is reflected back from the cloud by the water droplets that make it up. Like tiny prisms, these water droplets also refract the reflected light into the familiar colors of the rainbow. You see the rainbow effect as a colored halo around your shadow. You don't believe that's your shadow? Wave your arms and watch the shadow follow suit. Worldwide, seeing the Brocken specter used to be rare; nowadays, airline passengers frequently see the Brocken specter from the airplane. Still, it's much more exciting when the rainbow-circled shadow is yours, not the airplane's! The phenomenon is named for Brocken Mountain in Germany, where it was first described.

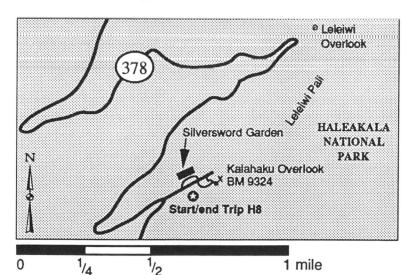

0   1/4   1/2   1 mile

Trip H8. Kalahaku Overlook.

Trip H9. White Hill

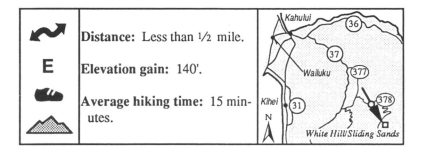

Distance: Less than ½ mile.	
E	Elevation gain: 140'.
	Average hiking time: 15 minutes.

Topos: *Kilohana* 7½.

Trail map (route approximated): At the end of this trip.

Highlights: The awesome panorama from the top of White Hill is something you won't forget. White Hill's summit is one of the favored places for watching sunrise at Haleakala, too. So is the Visitor Center, but it's usually crowded with those who came unprepared to wait in the icy dark. The vigil demands plenty of warm, windproof clothing—don't forget that warm hat and those gloves or mittens, either.

Driving instructions: Follow the driving instructions of Trip H3 past the Halemauu Trail turnoff and continue up the highway to the Visitor Center at White Hill, 40⅓ miles from Wailuku.

Permit/permission required: None.

Description: The trail up White Hill begins near the Visitor Center building, to its right as you face the building from the parking lot. It's a gentle but rocky grade; if you're coming here in the frigid predawn darkness, you'll need a flashlight to keep yourself on the trail and to avoid tripping over the rocks. The trail winds almost 360° around the hill as it rises to the summit, where a few tough dubautias live. From here, you have superb views in all directions once it's light. To the southwest sits Haleakala's high point, Red Hill (Trip H17). Southeast, you look over the crater walls to the summits of Mauna Kea and Mauna Loa on the Big Island of Hawaii, many miles away across the ocean. To the west, you have amazing views of the Isthmus and West Maui. And below you to the east, steep cliffs fall away into the crater. Perhaps the crater is clear of mist and dramatic with its cinder cones and sheer walls, or perhaps it's filled with clouds through which the cones push their dark heads. Nothing but the thin air separates you from the crater, making you feel almost as if you had wings and were soaring high above it.

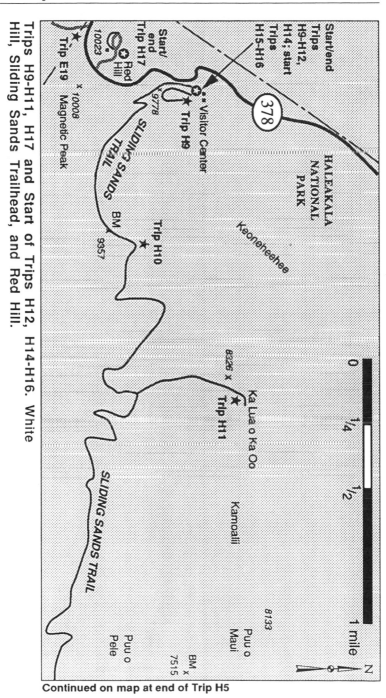

Trips H9-H11, H17 and Start of Trips H12, H14-H16. White Hill, Sliding Sands Trailhead, and Red Hill.

Continued on map at end of Trip H5

Trip H10. Sliding Sands Trail to "Rock Garden"

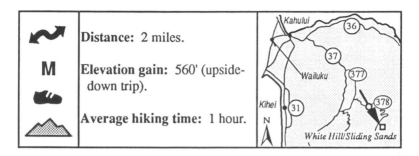

Distance: 2 miles.

M

Elevation gain: 560' (upside-down trip).

Average hiking time: 1 hour.

Topos: *Kilohana* 7½.

Trail map: At the end of Trip H9.

Highlights: This relatively short descent on the famous Sliding Sands Trail offers you a chance to experience hiking in Haleakala's crater and to enjoy some wonderful crater views.

Driving instructions: Follow the driving instructions of Trip H9. The Sliding Sands Trail is on the side of the parking lot nearer the highway (away from the Visitor Center building).

Permit/permission required: None.

Description: Pause at the trailhead sign to read its information and to pick up one of the park's brochures on hiking trails. Now that you're fully informed, follow the path away from the parking lot, briefly paralleling the highway. You're at the crater rim in a little over ⅛ mile. You can't help but pause and think, *How vast and life-less the crater seems from here!* Ahead, the Sliding Sands Trail stretches away along the cindery crater wall, dwindling till it seems little more than a scratch in the dark sand. Specks moving on the distant scratch will turn out to be your fellow hikers. Down in the crater, clouds drift in and out among the brown and red hulks of distant cinder cones, constantly changing the view. Far, far away at the east end of the crater, Kaupo Gap breaks the stark crater walls, mists ebbing and flowing through it. Perhaps you had thought you could easily orient yourself here; now, the crater's immensity may seem almost intimidating and its shifting clouds may defy your attempts to positively identify the landmarks that seemed so obvious from the Visitor Center.

The well-graded trail is pleasant walking, and you're soon descending, negotiating a couple of switchbacks, and looking forward to your next photo stop. You presently drop into the shallow depression between a low ridge on your left and the crater wall. At the next switchback, just under 1 mile from your start, you come upon a handsome formation of red-brown rock around which grow a number of bright green shrubs with cheery little puffs of yellow flowers. This striking natural arrangement of forms and colors is what I've called the "rock garden." These are dubautias, specifically dubautia menziesii, one of the plants most characteristic of this arid landscape (more about them below). Other dubautias grow in and around Haleakala, but this particular one, with its small, stiff, succulent leaves arranged rather formally in fours, is especially conspicuous because it seeks no shelter, growing instead in the most exposed places. A few stunted *pukiawe*, another hardy native shrub, grow here, too, but the dubautias are really the show.

When you're ready, retrace your steps.

Dubautias and their relatives. . . . Botanists believe that the endemic dubautias (*Dubautia*) and their showier endemic relatives, the silverswords (*Argyroxiphium*) and *iliau* (*Wilkesia*), share a common ancestor with the present-day tarweeds of California. The common California tarweed is a daisy-like annual plant, not particularly showy, competing with many other mainland species for survival and having few opportunities to radiate into different environmental niches.

The tarweeds that reached Hawaii, probably as bristly seeds stuck to birds' feathers, have undergone one of the most amazing adaptive radiations to be found in the Hawaiian Islands. As their common ancestor was adapted to dry locations, it's not surprising to find dubautias, silverswords, and *iliau* in arid places. But many dubautias have evolved into shrubs and trees of the rainforests. One dubautia even grows on the summit of Kauai's Mt. Waialeale, possibly the rainiest spot on earth. Another rare dubautia is a vine in Kauai's *koa* forests.

The Haleakala silversword occupies the extremely arid, bright alpine environment. The Kau silversword grows in a moist region on the slopes of Mauna Loa on the Big Island of Hawaii. More amazing still are the silverswords and greenswords (like silverswords but lacking silvery hairs) that grow in bogs like the one on Puu Kukui, the highest point on West Maui and another of the rainiest spots on earth.

The shrubby dubautias and the rosette-shaped silverswords are so closely related that they can hybridize naturally. *Plants and Flowers of Hawai'i* includes a photograph of one such natural hybrid, between the *Dubautia menziesii* you see here at the "rock garden" and the Haleakala silversword, *Argyroxiphium sandwicense*.

The *iliau*, one of only two members of its genus, occupies a moderately dry, scrubby forest niche around Waimea Canyon on Kauai. It's rare, but it doesn't seem to be an endangered species.

Apparently, the only major environmental niche the dubautia-silversword-*iliau* family doesn't occupy in the Hawaiian Islands is the lower coastal region—but it's one of the principal niches occupied by their California tarweed relatives and their presumed common ancestor. Perhaps that niche was already fully occupied when the ancestor of the dubautia-silversword-*iliau* family arrived, so the adaptable family went on to evolve into forms that occupy virtually every other niche in Hawaii.

Dubautia

Silversword

Trip H11. Sliding Sands Trail to Ka Lua o Ka Oo

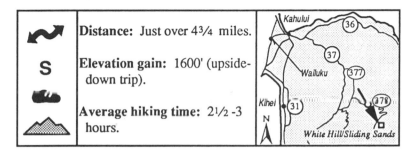

Distance: Just over 4¾ miles.

S

Elevation gain: 1600' (upside-down trip).

Average hiking time: 2½ -3 hours.

Topos: *Kilohana* 7½.

Trail map: At the end of Trip H9.

Highlights: Ka Lua o Ka Oo ("Kalua O Ka Oo" on the topo, "Ka Luu o ka Oo" on a park brochure) is one of the most colorful cones in the crater. The way it's tucked into the steep ridge below Red Hill means there's very little climbing required to get to its top. As a bonus, the spur trail from the Sliding Sands Trail to Ka Lua O Ka Oo presently has one of the best concentrations of silverswords to be found in the crater, several growing so near the trail that there's no excuse or need for stepping off the trail to get your own silversword photograph. A park brochure may be available for this hike; check at the trailhead. It says that "Ka Luu o ka Oo" means "the plunge [*luu*] of the digging-stick [*oo*]."

Driving instructions: Follow the driving instructions of Trip H9.

Permit/permission required: None.

Description: Follow the Sliding Sands Trail down to the "rock garden" as described in Trip H10. Continue down the ridge, where views of the crater open up again as you switchback away from the "rock garden." Silverswords appear along the trail as you approach the junction with the spur trail to Ka Lua o Ka Oo. The junction is set amid jagged lava formations, and you turn left (north) here toward the cone.

The spur trail makes a short, steep, rough descent at first. Then it levels out and curves around the steep but shallow depression below Red Hill and White Hill, revealing a landscape of red-brown cinders enlivened by the shining gray-white of silversword rosettes and the sprightly green of dubautia shrubs. Climbing a little, the spur trail leads right to the edge of the cone, from which a trail-of-use bears left around the cone's deep, brightly colored vent. Bluish-gray rocks dot the scene, and splashes of mineral colors stain the vent's throat and edges: reds, pinks, tans, blacks, oranges, golds, yellows, chocolates, and lavenders. Oh, for a wide-angle lens to capture all these wonderful colors at once!

As you enjoy this spectacle, Haleakala's clouds may drift in and drizzle on you, then float out, leaving the cone awash in sunlight, then swirl in again. Photography hint: in *Haleakala: A Guide to the Mountain*, the authors advise shutterbugs to meter off the ground, not off the too-bright sky, to avoid underexposures of crater scenery.

Too soon, it's time to return the way you came—almost all up-hill now—to your car.

Meadow and cinder cones west of Kapalaoa cabin

Trip H12. Sliding Sands to Kapalaoa Cabin
Dayhike or Backpack

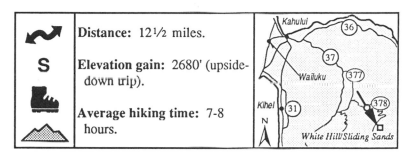

Distance: 12½ miles.

Elevation gain: 2680' (upside-down trip).

Average hiking time: 7-8 hours.

Topos: *Kilohana, Nahiku 7½.*

Trail map: Begins on the map at the end of Trip H9; ends on the map at the end of Trip H5.

Highlights: All the visual delights of Trips H10 and H11, plus a visit to Kapalaoa Cabin's tiny oasis. Crater views on the way back from Kapalaoa Cabin are especially stunning. I've described this trip as a dayhike, but you can also do it as a backpack if you can get a reservation for Kapalaoa Cabin.

Driving instructions: Follow the driving instructions of Trip H9.

Permit/permission required: None for dayhike. Required for an overnight stay at Kapalaoa Cabin (by reservation only); see Appendix A. There is no campground at Kapalaoa Cabin, so it's the cabin or nothing.

Description: Follow Trip H11 to Ka Lua O Ka Oo, but on your return to the junction with the Sliding Sands Trail, turn left and continue east down the trail. You come around some rocks to see wonderful colors on the adjacent hillsides—pinks, reds, and lavenders. As Puu o Pele looms ahead, you pass through an area of silverswords and presently begin hiking over rocks—chunks of *aa*—instead of the cinders you've been on till now. This area, which appears to be a dull, dark, monochrome from above, reveals itself to be full of subtle colors and intriguing textures. The view back up the Sliding Sands Trail from here is very striking.

You bear east-southeast past heaps of brick-red cinder near the top of Puu o Pele, then zigzag down, down, down its sides to a junction with the westernmost spur trail going north to Holua Cabin/Campground and the Halemauu Trail. Dark-brown Puu o Maui, the highest cone in the crater, is off to the north on one side of the spur trail, reddish Ka Moa o Pele on the other. South of you, on the crater walls, there's a patch of bracken fern. When it turns orange-gold in the fall, you may wonder if you've stumbled upon a field of California poppies in bloom. Here, 4 miles from your start, you bear right (ahead) toward Kapalaoa Cabin.

An unexpected delight, an alpine meadow of tussock grasses, grows along the Sliding Sands Trail between here and Kapalaoa Cabin. As you continue east, Ka Moa o Pele recedes, and you're able to see Halalii, Puu Naue, and Puu Nole cones to the north. You pass two more junctions with spur trails northward to Holua Cabin/ Campground and the Halemauu Trail, but you persist eastward to Kapalaoa Cabin. The third junction is only 1Z10 mile from Kapalaoa Cabin, which is perched on a small, grassy platform just south of the trail, dwarfed by the scrub-covered pali rising behind it. A picnic table, pit toilet, and water are available here, a little over 5¾ miles from your start (6½ miles if you detoured to see Ka Lua o Ka Oo). It's a wonderful place to rest, enjoy your lunch, and take in the awesome crater views. Resist the temptation to share your lunch with the engaging and shameless nene beggars here!

Retrace your steps to White Hill when you must; be sure to allow plenty of time for the steep pull up the hill.

Did the old Hawaiians come up to Haleakala crater? . . . There's no evidence that anyone ever lived permanently high on Haleakala or down in its crater, but there are ruins of stone shelters that the old Hawaiians used for temporary shelter while they were up here. The Hawaiians found the necessities of life in the ocean, on the coastal plains, and on the lower mountain slopes, not in the alien harshness of this high mountain. Yet there's plenty of evidence that the upper slopes and crater of Haleakala were ceremonially and economically important. The note at the end of Trip H7 mentioned the *heiau* on Haleakala peak. A survey of Haleakala (Emory, 1921, reported by Kirch in *Feathered Gods and Fishhooks*) lists "[58] terraces and platforms . . . , [9] groups of open stone shelters, 'several hundred' cairns, and a section of an ancient paved road. . . . Several of the terraces and cairns proved to contain burials." Slingstones found on the crater floor suggest that the Hawaiians came up here to hunt birds. They also came to Haleakala to mine its outcrops of fine-grained basalt, which was an excellent material for making adzes (cutting tools used chiefly for shaping wood). Radiocarbon dating of charcoal from one of the stone shelters shows people were here perhaps as early as the eighth century. The ancient paved road, which once connected Wailuku and Hana but has almost disappeared now, may indicate that the Hawaiians preferred the arduous climb up and down Haleakala to the tortuous coastal routes.

Trip H13. Kapalaoa Cabin Side Trip to Holua Cabin/Campground

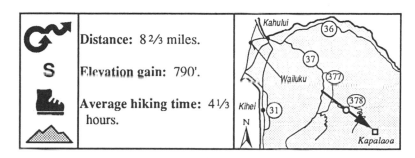

Distance: 8 2/3 miles.

Elevation gain: 790'.

Average hiking time: 4 1/3 hours.

Topos: *Kilohana, Nahiku* 7½.
Trail map: At the end of Trip H5.
Highlights: Many of the same scenic joys that highlight Trip H5 highlight this trip, too. However, this trip returns to Kapalaoa Cabin on the westernmost of the three maintained spur trails between the Sliding Sands and Halemauu trails. The return leg, passing between Puu o Maui and Ka Moa o Pele, offers a different experience of the crater floor from that offered by Trip H5.
Driving instructions: Not applicable.
Permit/permission required: None for this dayhike. Required to stay at Kapalaoa Cabin (see Trip H12 and Appendix A).
Description: From Kapalaoa Cabin, retrace your steps ⅓ mile west to the junction with the middle (second) maintained spur trail linking the Sliding Sands and Halemauu trails, as described in Trip H5. Follow this spur trail northwest to the saddle between Ka Moa o Pele and Halalii as described in the next-to-last paragraph of Trip H5. (I've chosen this spur trail because it offers such a stunning view of Ka Moa o Pele's vent as you walk it this direction.)

On the saddle, go right on the spur trail that heads around the east side of Halalii—uninteresting until it meets the Halemauu Trail on the saddle between Halalii and Puu Naue at the Bottomless Pit in Pele's Paint Pot. Turn left (west) on the Halemauu Trail through the dazzling colors of Pele's Paint Pot and follow it west and then northwest to the Silversword Loop, reversing part of the description of Trip H5. You can pick up the Silversword Loop now or on your way back from Holua Cabin/Campground. Continue northwest, still reversing Trip H5's description, to Holua Cabin/Campground. The scenery opens westward before you, and the meadow below Holua Cabin contrasts sharply with the forbidding lava wilderness you're traversing.

After enjoying your lunch at beautiful Holua Cabin, retrace your steps to the junction where the Halemauu Trail turns left (east) toward Pele's Paint Pot. Here, you bear right, past Pele's Pig Pen. At the junction just beyond Pele's Pig Pen, you turn sharply right and begin climbing the northern slopes of Ka Moa o Pele to a saddle between it and an unnamed cone to its north. Enjoy the view from this saddle before descending west and then southwest on the red slopes of Ka Moa o Pele. The dark brown slopes of Puu o Maui rise on your right (west). As the trail levels out, you enter a choppy, frozen "sea" of lava whose stony waves have crests of gray and orange rock and troughs of black sand.

You leave the lava "sea" behind as you approach a junction with the Sliding Sands Trail, where bracken, *mamane,* and yellow-flowered, alien evening primrose grow. At this junction, turn left (east) onto the Sliding Sands Trail and follow it back to Kapalaoa Cabin as described in Trip H12 to end a satisfying and highly varied hike.

Ideally. . . . you'd stay *two* nights at Kapalaoa Cabin to enjoy this side trip at a leisurely pace. If you can't get a permit for two nights, an alternative is to get an early start, stash most of your gear at Kapalaoa Cabin, take this side trip with a daypack, and pack out when you get back to Kapalaoa Cabin—before the next party arrives, you hope. Another choice, if you can get the necessary permit, is a backpacking variation on Trip H15: backpack down the Sliding Sands Trail as far as Kapalaoa Cabin, take one of these lovely spur trails to Holua Cabin/Campground (where you'll stay), and then pack out on the Halemauu Trail. However you manage it, I hope you won't miss the beauty of the central crater.

Kapalaoa cabin

Trip H14. Sliding Sands Trail to Paliku Cabin/Campground

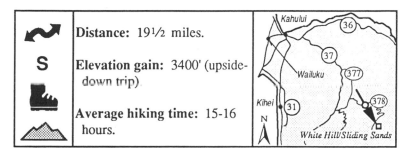

Distance: 19½ miles.	
Elevation gain: 3400' (upside-down trip).	
Average hiking time: 15-16 hours.	

Topos: *Kilohana, Nahiku* 7½.

Trail map: Begins on the map at the end of Trip H9; continues on the map at the end of Trip H5; ends on the map at the end of Trip H6.

Highlights: The beauty of the Sliding Sands Trail is yours to enjoy until, at Olii Puu, you pick up the Halemauu Trail for the different, but equally beautiful, stretch to Paliku Cabin/Campground.

Driving instructions: Follow the driving instructions of Trip H9.

Permit/permission required: Required for an overnight stay at Kapalaoa or Paliku Cabin or both (by reservation only) or at the campground adjacent to Paliku Cabin; see suggestions at the end of this trip and details in Appendix A.

Description (strenuous trip):

Day 1 (9¾ miles). Follow Trip H12 to Kapalaoa Cabin. On this trip, you can skip the detour to Ka Lua o Ka Oo (add just under 1 mile out and back and 150' elevation gain if you're determined to see it).

After a rest on Kapalaoa Cabin's lawn, you continue east on the Sliding Sands Trail into scrub country, where you soon begin a gentle descent as the trail bears northeast. Puu Maile, visible to the northeast when you left Kapalaoa, is soon hidden by a ridge of *aa*, and there's a dry wash to the southeast. The trail presently levels out amid rocks some of which are a lovely soft, dark, pinkish-red color. The trail becomes dusty as it passes through more scrub and bracken.

It's not long before Oili Puu comes into view ahead to the northeast as you descend moderately to steeply over some fairly stable rocks and through a region of scrub and jagged vents. A few curious little "buttes" stand a few feet above the general terrain here. A couple of them seem to be the products of spatter lava, but one, standing north of the trail and isolated in a flow of *pahoehoe*, appears to be a tiny columnar basalt formation (see Trip E10 for a discussion of this type of formation).

Your descent becomes more gradual as Paliku's meadow becomes visible to the east, only to be hidden by Oili Puu as you begin crossing a broad lava field. Ridges of *aa* are separated by narrow channels of green scrub—mostly *aalii, ohelo,* and *pukiawe.* Kaupo Gap opens on your right (east), but the challenge of negotiating the loose *aa* may keep you from appreciating it.

You leave the lava field on cinders dotted by *pukiawe* and evening primrose and shortly reach the junction of the Halemauu and Sliding Sands trails. Turn right (northeast) here at the foot of scrub-covered Oili Puu and follow Trip H6 to Paliku Cabin/Campground.

Day 2 (9¾ miles). Retrace your steps to the Sliding Sands trailhead.

Logistics. . . . The easier way to do this trip is to stay a night at Kapalaoa Cabin. If you want to stay overnight at Kapalaoa Cabin and can get a reservation for it, your trip will probably be easier if you backpack in directly to Paliku Cabin/Campground (downhill) and then stay at Kapalaoa Cabin on your way *out* (uphill).

Paliku cabin

Trip H15. Sliding Sands Trail to Halemauu Trail Adventure

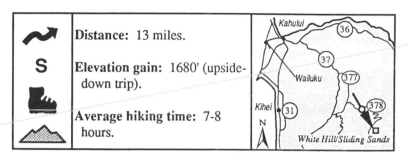

	Distance: 13 miles.
S	Elevation gain: 1680' (upside-down trip).
	Average hiking time: 7-8 hours.

Topos: *Kilohana, Nahiku* 7½.

Trail map: Begins on the map at the end of Trip H9; continues on the map at the end of Trip H5; ends on the map at the end of Trip H2.

Highlights: This is, I believe, the single finest dayhike in Haleakala's crater—make that the single finest dayhike on Maui. It's as complete a crater adventure as you can enjoy without staying overnight in the crater. By all means allow time for detours to Ka Lua o Ka Oo, the Bottomless Pit and Pele's Paint Pot, and the Silversword Loop! Take plenty of color film, and budget your time so that you can take advantage of the multitude of photo opportunities along the way.

Note that while this trip is described as a dayhike, you can also do it as a backpack if you can get permission to stay at Holua Cabin/Campground.

Driving instructions: This trip is a shuttle, so leave one car at the Halemauu Trail by following the driving instructions of Trip H3. Then, following the driving instructions of Trip H9, drive to White Hill to start your adventure at the Sliding Sands Trail.

Permit/permission required: None if done as a dayhike. See Appendix A for information on cabins and camping in the crater.

Description: Follow Trip H12 down the Sliding Sands Trail, detouring to visit Ka Lua o Ka Oo, to the junction with the first of the three maintained spur trails to the Halemauu Trail, 4¾ miles including the detour. Here, with Puu o Pele above you to the west and with Ka Moa o Pele ahead of you to the northeast, you turn left (northeast) onto the spur trail through the bracken, mamane, and evening primrose that grow around this junction.

Follow the spur trail northeast and then east, reversing part of

Trip H13, through the choppy lava "sea" and up the red slopes of Ka Moa o Pele. You descend to the point just east of and above Pele's Pig Pen on the saddle between Ka Moa o Pele and Halalii. Turn right and follow the trail around Halalii, going left at the next junction, to the Bottomless Pit. Turn left (west) onto the Halemauu Trail at the Bottomless Pit for a short walk through the intensely colorful area called Pele's Paint Pot.

At the next junction, on the west side of Halalii, you turn right (northwest) toward the Silversword Loop and Holua Cabin/Campground. Now you reverse the steps of part of Trip H5, detouring to see the Silversword Loop if you wish. The amount of vegetation increases as you rise toward Holua Cabin/Campground, where you'll welcome a chance to rest. All too soon, the pressure of time obliges you to resume your trip, reversing the steps of Trip H4 down the ridge, across the meadow, and up Leleiwi *Pali* to the crater rim.

At the crater rim viewpoint that's the destination for Trips H2 and H3, you can't help but pause for one final, long look at the stupendous world of Haleakala's crater. Continuing, you now enjoy views downslope to East Maui's north coast on your way to the Halemauu trailhead and your shuttle car. *Nene* at the parking lot hurry over to moo at you for a handout—no respect for the long-distance hiker *here!*—as you shed your pack, change into tennies, and ease your weary body into the car.

Sure, you're tired. But what's being tired compared to being dazzled by Haleakala's splendors?!

Shuttle, anyone? . . . How do you set up a shuttle for a group that's sharing just one rental car? It's easy if you've made sure your group includes at least one non-hiker who doesn't mind driving the hikers around. Perhaps that's not so easy. Other options: rent another car for the necessary period; take the trip with an organized group whose arrangements include the shuttle; or, if you have friends on Maui, arrange for one of them to pick you up.

But let's assume you're limited to one car and have no other options. What if everyone wants to hike? What if there's only the one of you? Forget taking the trip as a shuttle. Instead, select a midpoint along the trip and take an out-and-back hike from each end of it to your midpoint. This has some real advantages: You get to enjoy the trip twice as much; you won't have to make any complicated arrangements; you won't have to hold yourself to a schedule for meeting a ride; and you won't keep anyone waiting and worrying at the other end.

Trip H16. Grand Crater Tour (Backpack)

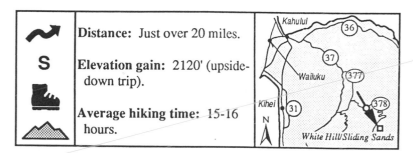

Distance: Just over 20 miles.

Elevation gain: 2120' (upside-down trip).

Average hiking time: 15-16 hours.

Topos: *Kilohana, Nahiku 7½.*

Trail map: Begins on the map at the end of Trip H9; continues on the maps at the end of Trips H5 and H6; ends on the map at the end of Trip H2.

Highlights: You see virtually every one of the finest crater features that maintained trails take you to. On the way, you sample the comforts of the cabins or campgrounds, or both, depending on the mix of reservations and permits you're able to get. The easiest trip, described below, is possible only if you can get a reservation for Kapalaoa Cabin for your first night. Otherwise, combine Days 1 and 2 to go directly to Paliku Cabin/Campground on your Day 1 as described in Trip H14, and consider spending two nights at Paliku Cabin/Campground. That would allow you to take Trip H7, too.

Driving instructions: This trip is a shuttle like Trip H15, whose driving instructions you should follow.

Permit/permission required: Required for an overnight stay at any of the cabins (by reservation only) or at the campgrounds adjacent to Paliku and Holua cabins; see Appendix A.

Description (easiest trip):

Day 1 (just over 5¾ miles). Follow Trip H12 from the Sliding Sands trailhead to Kapalaoa Cabin.

Day 2 (4 miles). Follow Trip H14 from Kapalaoa Cabin to Paliku Cabin/Campground.

Day 3 (6⅓ miles). Reverse the steps of Day 2 of Trip H6 from Paliku Cabin/Campground to Holua Cabin/Campground.

Day 4 (just under 4 miles). Reverse the steps of Trip H4 from Holua Cabin/Campground to the Halemauu trailhead. Early birds will find that it's possible to take Trip H5 before packing out.

Trip H17. Red Hill Minihike

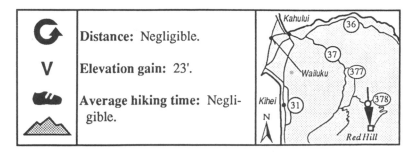

Distance: Negligible.

Elevation gain: 23'.

Average hiking time: Negligible.

Topos: Optional: *Kilohana* 7½.
Trail map (route approximated): At the end of Trip H9.
Highlights: Red Hill (Puu Ulaula), 10,023 feet high, is the highest point on Haleakala and, therefore, on Maui. The parking lot itself is at 10,000 feet! The views from Red Hill are superb. The air is pretty thin at this altitude, so take it easy. Make this an early morning visit so that the cloud bank that normally forms by midmorning won't obstruct your view.
Driving instructions: Follow the driving instructions of Trip H9 past the Visitor Center turnoff at White Hill and continue all the way up Highway 378 past the turnoff to Science City to the parking lot for the observation shelter at the very top of Haleakala.
Permit/permission required: None.
Description: From the parking lot, climb the stairs to the enclosed observation shelter, where marked stations point out features of the nearly–360° view from here. Mauna Kea and Mauna Loa on the Big Island of Hawaii, many miles away to the south-southeast, are particularly striking from Red Hill. Magnetic Peak, right next door in the southeast, is reputed to be so full of iron that it interferes with compass readings. The view southwest and west over Science City, the Isthmus, and West Maui is unparalleled.

The sight of Science City is even more striking from outside the shelter, so follow the little path outside the shelter. The white domes and buildings of Science City and the barren red-brown clinker of Haleakala's summit region combine to make a landscape so stark, so surreal, and so alien that you may think you've strayed onto the set of a science-fiction movie or been translated to Mars like Edgar Rice Burroughs's hero John Carter. But please don't step off the path. Despite its apparent lifelessness, there is life in this harsh environment, and a careless step can too easily crush seedlings and tiny creatures hidden in the clinker.

From here, take the other stairs down to the parking lot and return to your car.

Skyline Trail. . . . Remember that you can reverse the directions for the Skyline Trail, Trip E19 in this book, and take it from Science City, just below Red Hill. That will make it an upside-down trip, but getting to the Skyline Trail from Science City rather than from Polipoli will be more practical for many people, because the road to Polipoli is awful, while the road to Red Hill is quite good.

Your best bet is probably to leave your car parked here at Red Hill and *carefully* walk back down the road to the turnoff for Science City. The Skyline Trail branches off from the Science City road just a little past the National Park boundary sign. This would add ¾ mile and 100 feet of elevation gain to your Skyline Trail hike or mountain-bicycle trip. You could more than compensate for that by turning around at Ballpark Junction instead of going all the way to Polipoli. Sturdy cyclists who can set up the shuttle may be interested in continuing all the way down from Polipoli to Highway 377 and meeting their shuttle ride in Kula.

Cones in Haleakala Crater. Mauna Kea and Mauna Loa in the distance.

Bibliography

Beckwith, Martha. *Hawaiian Mythology*. New Haven: Yale University Press (for the Folklore Foundation of Vassar College), 1940. Reprint. Honolulu: University of Hawaii Press, 1970, 1976.

Bisignani, J.D. *Hawaii Handbook*. 2nd ed. Chico, California: Moon Publications, Inc., 1989.

Carlquist, Sherwin. *Hawaii, A Natural History.* 2nd ed., 2nd printing. Lawai, Kauai: National [formerly Pacific] Tropical Botanical Garden, 1980, 1985.

Chisolm, Craig. *Hawaiian Hiking Trails.* 3rd ed. Lake Oswego, Oregon: The Fernglen Press, 1989.

Clark, John. *Hawaii's Secret Beaches, A Guide to Twenty-Four Hawaiian Beaches.* Honolulu: Tongg Publishing.

Day, A. Grove, and Carl Stroven, Eds. *A Hawaiian Reader.* Appleton-Century-Crofts, 1959. Reprint. Honolulu: Mutual Publishing Company, 1984.

Day, A. Grove. *Hawaii and Its People.* New York: Duell, Sloan and Pearce, 1955.

Epidemiology Branch, State Department of Health, State of Hawaii. "Leptospirosis in Hawaii." October 1, 1987.

Fleming, Martha Foss. *Old Trails of Maui.* Sponsored by William & Mary Alexander Chapter, Daughters of the American Revolution, 1933. (Obtained through the courtesy of Mr. Don Reeser, Superintendent, Haleakala National Park.)

Hargreaves, Dorothy, and Bob Hargreaves. *Hawaii Blossoms.* Japan: Dorothy and Bob Hargreaves, 1958. Reprint. Lahaina: Ross-Hargreaves.

———. Tropical Trees of Hawaii. Kailua: Hargreaves Company.

Hawai'i Audubon Society. *Hawaii's Birds.* 4th ed. Honolulu: Hawai'i Audubon Society, 1989.

Hill, Mary. *Geology of the Sierra Nevada.* Berkeley: University of California Press, 1975.

Joesting, Edward. *Hawaii, An Uncommon History.* New York: W.W. Norton & Company Inc., 1972.

Kepler, Angela Kay. *Maui's Hana Highway, A Visitor's Guide.* Honolulu: Mutual Publishing Company, 1987.

Kepler, Cameron B., and Angela Kay Kepler. *Haleakala: A Guide to the Mountain.* Honolulu: Mutual Publishing Company, 1988.

Kirch, Patrick Vinton. *Feathered Gods and Fishhooks: An Introduction to Hawaiian Archaeology and Prehistory.* Honolulu: University of Hawaii Press, 1985.

Kyselka, Will, and Ray Lanterman. *Maui: How It Came To Be.* Honolulu: University of Hawaii Press, 1980.

Levi, Herbert W., and Lorna R. Levi. *Spiders and their Kin.* New York: Golden Press, 1987.

Macdonald, Gordon A., Agatin T. Abbott, and Frank L. Peterson. *Volcanoes in the Sea, the Geology of Hawaii.* 2nd ed. Honolulu: University of Hawaii Press, 1986.

Mack, Jim. *Haleakala: the Story Behind the Scenery.* 4th printing. Las Vegas: KC Publications, 1979.

Merlin, Mark David. *Hawaiian Coastal Plants and Scenic Shorelines.* 3rd printing. Honolulu: Oriental Publishing Co., 1986.

————. *Hawaiian Forest Plants.* 3rd ed. Honolulu: The Oriental Publishing Co., 1980.

Mrantz, Maxine. *Women of Old Hawaii.* Honolulu: Aloha Publishing, 1975.

Pukui, Mary Kawena, Samuel H. Elbert, and Esther T. Mookini. *The Pocket Hawaiian Dictionary.* Honolulu: University of Hawaii Press, 1975.

Smith, Rodney N. *Hawaii: A Walker's Guide.* Edison, New Jersey: Hunter Publishing, Inc.

Sohmer, S.H., and R. Gustafson. *Plants and Flowers of Hawai'i.* Honolulu: University of Hawaii Press, 1987.

Winnett, Thomas, and Melanie Findling. *Backpacking Basics.* 3rd ed. Berkeley: Wilderness Press, 1988.

Woolliams, Keith. *A Guide to Hawaii's Popular Trees.* 2nd ed. Aiea, Hawaii: Island Heritage Publishing, 1988.

Zurick, David. *Hawaii, Naturally.* Berkeley: Wilderness Press, 1990.

Appendix A. Camping on Maui

Backcountry camping accessible on foot. Backcountry camping that's accessible only on foot is practical for the tourist from the mainland only in Haleakala crater (Haleakala National Park). You must have a permit to stay in the campgrounds or cabins in the crater. You may *not* camp in the crater outside of the campgrounds or cabins. Your stay in the crater is limited to 3 nights per month, whether in cabins or campgrounds or a combination of cabins and campgrounds. Your stay at any one location in the crater is limited to 2 consecutive nights; for this purpose, a cabin and its adjacent campground (if any) count as different locations.

Crater campgrounds. There are two tent-campgrounds in the crater, one near Holua Cabin (6960 feet) and the other near Paliku Cabin (6380 feet). Permits for tent camping in the crater are issued *only in person* at Park Headquarters (or, for very early starts before Park Headquarters opens, at the Visitor Center near the summit) and *only on the day you begin your trip.* There are quotas, so be prepared to modify your itinerary or come back another day if the quotas are filled. There is no fee. The crater can be cold (my thermometer read 40° F one clear morning after a rainy night at Holua Campground), windy, and rainy, so you must be prepared with a rainproof tent, warm clothes, rain gear, and a stove that you can start and keep going in wind and rain. A friend who thought he wouldn't need his whole tent in Hawaii and who went into Haleakala crater with only the rainfly for shelter was very sorry, very cold, and very soggy. The ranger who issues your permit will ask about your preparedness.

Crater cabins. There are three cabins in Haleakala Crater: Holua Cabin, Kapalaoa Cabin, and Paliku Cabin. Only one party as a unit may use a cabin at a time; a cabin holds up to 12 people. The cabins have tables, benches, bare bunkbeds (you'll still need your sleeping bag), and a kitchen with potable running water, a wood stove and wood (or those logs made from chips), and cooking and eating utensils. There is no electricity or lanterns; bring your flashlight and candle lantern. Each cabin also has an outhouse. Applying for a cabin is complicated. Currently, you must write to the Park Superintendent *at least 90 days in advance* of your trip (6–8 months

198

recommended), specifying your first and alternate choices of dates
and cabins preferred. As the park's brochure says, "The less restric-
tive your choice, the better your chance of confirmation." Just who
out of all the applicants will get to use a particular cabin on a particular day is decided by lottery. You will be notified by mail if you have
won the right to use a cabin. If you have won a reservation, you will
be required to pay a fee for each person in your party and to put a
deposit on the cabin key(s), which you must pick up at Park Headquarters on the day you begin your trip. Fees and deposits have
changed a lot recently; in October of 1990, I paid $17.50 for one night
for one person at Paliku Cabin plus a $15 key deposit.

People sometimes cancel their cabin reservations. It's remotely
possible that you'll get a night at a cabin just because you happen to
be at the Park Headquarters counter when someone cancels a
reservation. Don't count on it, though.

Haleakala National Park's address is:

Haleakala National Park
Box 369
Makawao, Maui, HI 96768
808-572-7749 (recording of general information); 808-572-9177
(recording of camping and cabin information); 808-572-9306 (park
headquarters; 7:30 A.M. to 4:00 P.M. Hawaii Standard Time).

Other (outside Haleakala). There are two other possibilities for
those who are desperate to do some backpacking, though these sites
are also accessible by 4WD vehicles. See the supplemental information following Trips E18 and E20.

Car camping. Maui doesn't offer much car camping—the
kind of camping where you drive up, pay your bucks, pick a space,
park your car, and pitch your tent there and live out of it (or live out
of your parked vehicle). For those who enjoy car camping, there is a
list below of the places you can car camp on Maui. This information
is largely from other sources, such as the agency in charge; I've veri-
fied the information for only a couple of these places.

Car camping at Haleakala National Park is limited to Hosmer
Grove (just off Highway 378, which goes to Haleakala crater's principal trailheads and to Haleakala's summit) and Kipahulu (the coastal
section of the park, south and west of Hana). No permit is required.
Camping is free. Camping at Hosmer Grove is limited to 25 persons
(organized groups are limited to 15 persons). However, there may be
no one to see that the limit is observed. The result may be that
Hosmer Grove, so peaceful by day, will be jammed full of people by
nightfall. Those who can't cram into the campground may try to
sleep in their cars along the road! A stay at Hosmer Grove may be

less than idyllic. Camping at Hosmer Grove and Kipahulu is limited to 3 nights per month. Trailers are permitted in the parking lot of Hosmer Grove. RVs are not permitted at either site.

Car camping at the state parks is by permit only and for a maximum of 5 consecutive nights in any 30-day period. Permits are free. They are issued Monday through Friday, 8 A.M. to 4 P.M., at the Division of State Parks office in Wailuku. The person appearing to apply for the permit must provide proper identification for each person in the party who is 18 years old or older. "Proper identification" means a driver's license or passport. You may also apply by mail at least seven days in advance of your proposed trip by writing to the Division of State Parks. When applying by mail, include a copy of the proper identification for each person in the party who is 18 years old or older. Trailers and RVs are not permitted in Maui's state parks. For the state parks, write or call:

> Department of Land and Natural Resources
> Division of State Parks, Maui District
> P.O. Box 1049
> Wailuku, Maui, HI 96793
> 808-244-4324 (or 808-244-4354 for camping and cabin reservations)

Car camping on Division of Forestry and Wildlife lands. At present, there are no car-campgrounds in areas managed by the Division of Forestry and Wildlife.

Car camping at Maui County's parks. Two of Maui County's parks allow car camping. It's limited to a maximum of 3 consecutive nights at one campsite. Permits are required. There is a fee per night: $3.00 per adult and 50¢ per child. Obtain permits by mail from:

> Department of Parks and Recreation, County of Maui
> 1580 Kaahumanu Avenue
> Wailuku, Maui, Hawaii 96793
> 808-243-7389

Private. Car camping is possible at one private campground, Camp Pecusa. This is an Episopalian Church campground on the beach at Olowalu, but they allow the general public to camp there for a fee as long as there's room. It's the only car-campground on West Maui. Write or call:

> Camp Pecusa
> 800 Olowalu Village
> Lahaina, HI 96761
> 808-661-4303

The following table summarizes the car-camping opportunities.

Name	Type	Nearest Town	Amenities; Restrictions
Hosmer Grove	National Park	Kula	Grills, tables, potable water, picnic pavilion, toilets. Tents only in campground proper; trailers permitted in parking lot. Rainy. Free. No permit required. Stays limited. At 6800'.
Kipahulu	National Park	Hana	Grills, toilets, and tables. No potable water. Tents only. Free. No permit required. Stays limited. Near sea level.
Waianapanapa	State	Hana	Potable water, picnic tables, outdoor showers, barbecue grills, toilets. Tents or campers. Free. Permit required. Stays limited. Near sea level.
Polipoli	State	Kula	Potable water, restroom, picnic tables, shelters. Tents only. Dark and rainy. Free. Permit required. Stays limited. At 6200'.
H.A. Baldwin	County	Paia	Restrooms and outdoor showers. Tents only. Fee. Permit required; see above. The camping area abuts the highway. *Hawaii, Naturally* recommends *against* a stay here. Stays limited. Sea level.
Rainbow Park	County	Paia	Restrooms. Tents only. Fee. Permit required; see above. Stays limited. Elevation unspecified; estimated at 800'.
Camp Pecusa	Private	Olo-walu	$3 per night per tent. No limit on stays. Only camping on West Maui. Sea level.

Cabins. The following areas offer cabins, which you should reserve (or try to reserve) months in advance.

Haleakala National Park. There are three backcountry cabins in Haleakala National Park in the crater. See "Backcountry camping accessible on foot" at the front of this section.

State parks. There are 12 cabins at Waianapanapa State Park (*very* popular) and one cabin at Polipoli State Park (popular). There is a fee per person per night, and your stay is limited to a maximum of 5 consecutive nights in any 30-day period. Write or call the state parks at the address or telephone number given above. I think the trail shelters in Polipoli are not worthy of your consideration; see the note following Trip E17.

Private. Camp Pecusa also has a few cabins, for which they charge a modest fee. Write the camp at the address given above or call the telephone number also given above.

Holua cabin in Haleakala crater

Appendix B. Hikes You Won't Find Here and Why

You may have read articles on the following hikes, seen them mentioned in other books, or noticed them on topos. Some of them are in this book but under different names. Some of these routes are closed because landowners no longer give permission to hike them. Others have become unsafe; I firmly believe that a vacation is not enhanced by a trip to the emergency room that you could have missed by avoiding a dangerous route. Finally, I judge that some are too remote and too boring to be worth your time.

West Maui/Isthmus

Iao Valley State Park—Poohahoahoa, Nakalaloa, and Kinihapai streams. A spur trail goes partway up Poohahoahoa Stream; see Trip W9. Otherwise, these are trailless; reputed to be difficult, rugged, and slippery where you have to walk in the streambed; subject to flash flooding.

Kealaloloa Ridge. The land has changed hands, according to the former owner's wife. A representative of the Division of Forestry and Wildlife told me that they now control access to the ridge but do not grant it for recreational hiking. I think that's just as well. As a practical matter, the trailhead is extremely hard to spot. The turnoff from Highway 30 to the trailhead is around a blind curve and onto a strip of dirt that's about one car long from the highway to the trailhead gate. In the fast and often heavy traffic that prevails around that turnoff, would you be more likely to get rear-ended or to crash into the gate?

Lahaina "L." See Trip W12 to David Malo's grave.

Puu Kukui. Closed to casual hikers. The Nature Conservancy now helps the landowner, the Maui Land and Pineapple Company, manage the swamps on the slopes and summit of Puu Kukui. Access is severely restricted, to protect rare native species, the ecosystem, and the watershed. The survival of endangered species and fragile ecosystems is much more important than the recreational wishes of our numerous and mobile species. We can so easily go somewhere else to hike—and just about anywhere else sounds better than Puu Kukui, anyway. One source describes Puu Kukui as having been "the most exhilarating and interesting" hike on Maui and describes the hiker's condition on this trail as ". . . soaked to the skin and chilled to the bone." Okay, all of you who came to Maui to get soaked to the skin and chilled to the bone, raise your hands! . . . That's what I thought. (Apparently, the reason for going to the top of Puu Kukui was to enjoy the views— views seldom available because of the cloud cover.)

Cross Above Wailuku. Wailuku Agribusiness no longer grants permission to hike to this landmark.

Huluhulupueo Stream. The bridge described as the starting point is over the Waihee River. Huluhulupueo Stream is a tributary of the Waihee River, joining it over a mile upriver from the bridge. I found no parking on or near the bridge. Access to the river from the bridge and highway is blocked by barbed wire, keep out signs, somebody's yard, and steep concrete abutments. Try Trips W2 and W9 for streamside hikes on West Maui.

East Maui (except for Haleakala National Park, which you'll find below)

Keanae Village. With all due respect to Keanae, the village isn't particularly interesting. I found a NO TRESPASSING sign between me and the one thing I thought *might* have been interesting. Also, if the people of Keanae wanted to make a tourist showplace of their village, there'd be signs on the highway inviting us to come on down and visit—but there aren't. There's a restroom near the end of the peninsula, and you might want to take some photos of the coast from there. That's about it.

Blue Pool. See Trip E5, Ulaino Road.

Hana Town. Hana isn't a particularly good "walking" town, as explained in Trip E11, because it's hilly, hot and humid, and lacks sidewalks. See Trips E11 and E12 for walks in Hana.

Helio's Grave. Trail reported to be too dangerous to hike on any more.

Polipoli State Park. With all due respect to the people of Maui, there is little at Polipoli State Park for the visitor from the mainland. See the discussion following Trip E17. About specific trails, alphabetically:

Boundary Trail. An oppressive, dark, and *very* dull trail made irritatingly hard to follow by the number of thoughtless trails-of-use that crisscross it. Northeastern part damaged by pigs and dirt bikes.

Haleakala Ridge Trail. Crisscrossed by trails-of-use; dull. See Polipoli Loop, below.

Kahua Road. Worthwhile. See Trip E18.

Mamani Trail. Apparently never constructed.

Plum Trail. Oppressive, dark, and dull. The plum trees have died from lack of light and from competition. See Polipoli Loop, below.

Polipoli Loop (Polipoli, Haleakala Ridge, Plum, and Redwood trails). This hike is an old standard, but I found it oppressive, dark, and dull. Here's a condensed description of it in case you have a lot of time to kill: Loop; moderate; tennis shoes okay; mountains, 3½ miles, 880' elevation gain (upside-down trip), 1¾ hours. This hike starts on the Polipoli Trail near the west edge of the campground. You leave the campground on that trail, under oppressive overgrowth, climb steeply but briefly to a 3-way junction, and turn right (west) onto what turns out to be the Haleakala Ridge Trail. The trail presently turns into the Plum Trail, which you follow past an intersection with the Tie Trail and past the abandoned Civilian Conservation Corps bunkhouse to a junction with the Boundary and Redwood trails. Turn right on the Redwood Trail and reverse the steps of Trip E17 back to the campground. You may want to take the Boundary Trail to the Fuchsia Wall before turning onto the Redwood Trail.

Polipoli Trail. Oppressive, dark and dull. See Polipoli Loop, above.

Redwood Trail. Oppressive, dark, and dull. Unlike any mainland stand of coast redwoods I've ever seen— and not a change for the better. See Trip E17 and Polipoli Loop, above.

Skyline Trail. Worthwhile. See Trip E19.

Tie Trail. Oppressive, dark, and dull.

Upper Waiakoa (Waiohuli) Trail. Severely damaged by feral pigs; impassable. The area is tagged, but the tags are worse than useless—they're misleading.

Waiakoa Loop Trail. Badly damaged by feral pigs; impassable after the first half-mile.

Puu Pimoe. Ulupalakua Ranch no longer gives permission to hike here.

Piiholo Hill. Haleakala Ranch no longer gives permission to hike here (they've leased it to another party who doesn't give permission, either).

Haleakala National Park

This book covers all the *maintained* trails in Haleakala National Park as Trips H1 through H17. (A number of trails that used to be maintained aren't any more and should be considered unsafe.) Particularly in the western part of the crater, the maintained trails represent the only environmentally safe way through a very fragile ecosystem. Safety—yours and the ecosystem's—dictates that you stick to the maintained trails. There are more than enough maintained trails in and around Haleakala to keep you busy, including enough crater trails to keep you hopping for the maximum 3 nights/4 days you can spend in the crater.

Nene **at Kapalaoa cabin**

Appendix C. How I Got Distances, Elevations, Times, and Trail Maps

I estimated distances primarily by time, knowing that I hike 2 miles/hour and backpack at 1⅓ miles/hour. I compared the distances I got by time with distance values supplied by the agencies in charge of the trails. In a few cases, I also had distance data from plots I'd made from the topos. When those distances were close, I felt satisfied with the distance I'd estimated by time. I usually rounded the distances off to the nearest ¼ or ⅓ mile.

I got most driving distances by rental-car odometer, which was consistent to within ±1/10 mile over routes I drove repeatedly. When I had not started from Wailuku, I added or subtracted the distance from my starting point to Wailuku. I found that in some cases I did not get usable odometer data; in those cases, I used data from the University of Hawaii Press map of Maui.

I determined elevation from topos and with an altimeter. Where I had altimeter data, I looked for close correspondence between those values, topo values, and any values supplied by the agency in charge of the trail.

Trail times are based on the time I actually spent in motion on the trail.

I made the trail maps by first scanning relevant pieces of the USGS topos into a computer. I put the resulting digitized topo information that applied to a trip or a set of trips into the bottom layer of a multiple-layer electronic drawing. I then traced selected topo information from the bottom layer onto a transparent electronic top layer. I hid the bottom layer containing the scanned data when I printed out the finished maps for this book. I left out the elevation contours because the resolution of the scanned data is too coarse to show the elevation contours and they would have taken me too long to draw. I added, deleted, or modified topo information that I knew had changed. My choices of conventions for trails, roads, boundaries, etc., primarily reflect the software's capabilities.

Many trails on Maui do not appear at all on the topos or in usable form on any official agency map. For them, I approximated the route based on field notes and sketches and any agency information I could find.

Index

Bailey House *See Maui Historical Society Museum*
Big Beach 142-43
black-sand beaches 100-01
Blue Pool *See Ulaino Road*
Bottomless Pit 165, 167
Boundary Trail 127, 205
Brocken specter 177
Brouillard, Ray 157

cabins 198-99, 202
campgrounds 198-201
camping, general 198-202
"cloud forest" hikes 152
Columbus, Christopher 14
Cook, Captain James 14-15
Cross Above Wailuku 204

Davis, Isaac 70-71
D.T. Fleming Beach Park 77-78
dubautias and their relatives 181-82

equipment suggestions, hints 28-32

Fagan, Paul 108
Findling, Melanie 28
Forestry and Wildlife, Division of 25
fretwork weathering 80

Haleakala
—, age of 11
—, origin of crater 1
—, weather 136-37
Haleakala National Park
—, address of 24, 199
—, cabins and camping in 199, 201-202
—, Kipahulu District of 2, 113-19
Haleakala Ridge Trail 205
Hale Hoikeike *See Maui Historical Society Museum*
Halekii-Pihana State Monument 48-50

Halemauu Trail 155-70, 187-88, 191-93
Hana
— Highway 20, 83, 86
— (town)
—, getting to 93-94
—, Hasegawa's General Store in 109-10
Hawaii Visitors Bureau 5
Hawaiian
— Islands
—, history 10-19
—, origin 10-11
— language 6-9, 18
— religion 13-15
Helio's Grave 204
Hoapili Trail 139-41
Hosmer Grove Nature Loop 150-52
Huluhulupueo Stream 204

Iao Needle, origin of 60
Iao Valley State Park 57-65

Kaahumanu 15-16, 109
Kahanu Gardens 94-95
Kahekili 55
Kahikinui Trail 132-33
Kahoolawe (island) 146
Kahua Road 131-33
Kalahaku Overlook 176-77
Kalanikupule 55-56
Ka Lua o Ka Oo 183-84
Kamaole County Beach Park 147-48
Kamehameha (I) 15, 55-56, 70-71
Kanaha Pond 52-53, 67
Kaupo Gap, Trail, village 21, 120-23, 172-73
Kealaloloa Ridge 203
Kealia Pond 67
Keanae Arboretum 88-89
Keanae Village 204
Kepaniwai, battle of 55-56
Kepaniwai County Park 54-56

208

Acknowledgements

For their encouragement, help, advice, and endless patience: alphabetically, Barbara Dallavo, Christina O'Keefe, and Thomas Winnett.

Also alphabetically, Jeff Bagshaw, Judy Visty, Ronald J. Nagata, and Don Reeser of Haleakala National Park generously gave their time, information, and advice. Bob Hobdy of the Division of Forestry and Wildlife, Maui District, answered many questions. Helen Downing of Kealia Condominiums always had a smile and a few minutes to spend giving advice from a local perspective.

For sending useful information to and answering endless questions from a total stranger: Division of Forestry and Wildlife, Maui District; Division of State Parks, Maui District; and the Hawaii Visitors Bureau, Los Angeles Office.

I hope I have accurately and adequately reflected the information these people, and many others, provided directly or indirectly. Any misunderstanding or errors are my responsibility.

K.M.